What Are the Readers Saying?

"I sat in my favorite over stuffed chair, legs up over the side and read "Dialogues with the Angels" every chance I had. I loved it! It brought me to tears and laughter, introspection and discovery again and again. A must read!"
Susanne "Shallinah" Konicov
Editor, "Connecting Link" Magazine

"Magical and enchanted ... This compelling spiritual journey will awaken thousands to the connection with their own Inner Guides. I could not put it down."
Karen Willis
Editor, "Aurora Magazine"

"It's been a long time since I couldn't put an manuscript down. Walking with Grace with your etherial entourage consciously at your side is very '90's. "Dialogues With the Angels" is a doorway into those places of knowing that allow our innocence to return us to Grace. Wonderful reading!"
Gary Bonnell
Author of "Ascension" and "Your Book of Life"

"Dialogues With the Angels" is a magic book! Through the gentle intermingling of tenderness and wisdom you awakened my soul and touched chords in my heart that continue to reverberate."
Lorin Zaret,
Healing Practitioner

"Your book is an inspiration! You trigger the cellular memory of who we really are. It is a cosmic roller coaster."
Nori Halpern
Dancer, visionary and wife

D1566198

Dialogues is one of those incredible books that virtually yells best seller! I challenge anyone to pick it up and not be moved. It struck deep into my heart.
David Ryback
Author of "Dreams That Come True"

"I love this book. It is like none other. Perhaps because it is so real and so honest. It is a masterpiece of the soul, birthed of the spirit, immersed in the heart. Sometimes I just put my hand on it to feel all that it embraces in my being."
Leslie Sherman
Writer and teacher

"A fabulous journey into the realm of angels through one woman's experience and search for angelic understanding. Enlightening, explorative and entertaining!"
Linda Vephula Light,
Editor "Angel Times" Magazine

"Provocative, intriguing and engaging! "Dialogues With the Angels" is an excellent bridge into the Spirit Realms. It causes the reader to reconsider their beliefs about angels, ETs, devas, gods, goddesses, and other spiritual beings. It has made me rethink how I relate to these spiritual dimensions."
Dan Liss
Editor, "Aquarius Newspaper"

"This journey is a search for truth. It is the story of a girl who wants to live with the immortals. It was so real it lived inside of me. I loved it!"
Hank Passafero
Theosophist & Bard

Dialogues with the Angels

Tricia McCannon

HORIZONS UNLIMITED, INC
ATLANTA, GEORGIA

First Edition

6/98

ISBN 1-886932-01-8

Library of Congress Catalog Card Number: 96-65892

Cover design: Greg Waters
Illustration: Jean Francois Podevin

Printed in the United States of America by Darby Printing Company
Printed on recycled paper.

Published by Horizons Productions Unlimited Inc.,
931 Monroe Drive, Suite 102 - #329
Atlanta, Georgia 30308

Dedication

To my Mother in Heaven
and my
Mother on Earth,
Both of whom have blessed
my life immeasurably
With their love

"Our birth is but a sleep and a forgetting,
The soul that rises with us, our life's star
Hath had elsewhere its setting,
And cometh from afar
Not in entire forgetfulness,
And not in utter nakedness,
But trailing clouds of glory do we come
From God, who is our home:
Heaven lies about us in our infancy
Shades of the prison-house begin to close
Upon the growing boy.
The youth, who daily farther from the east must travel
Still is Nature's priest
And by the vision splendid
Is on his way attended:
At length the man perceives it die away
And fade into the light of common day...

...Truths that wake,
To perish never.
Though inland far we be,
Our souls have sight of that immortal sea
Which brought us hither.

William Wordsworth from
*"Intimations of Immortality
from Recollections of Early Childhood"*

Grace In Childhood

The Search Begins

Descent Into The World

They Come As Angels

Stories from the Center

Prologue

I was raised in the deep south in a very conservative Christian household, yet I had memories of Angels from the time I was a child. I heard music playing in my head, felt nature spirits in the forests, and saw a host of "other worldly" things which did not quite fit into the neat, three-dimensional picture I was being taught. I did not know then that I was what many now call a clairvoyant, but I did know that there was more to the Universe than what traditional science and Judeo-Christian teachings allowed us to hear, and I was intent upon finding out what it was.

In fact, my senior year in high school my two best friends and I sat together on the steps outside of school a week before graduation day and asked each other what we wanted to do with our lives. Chris, the shy, retiring, brilliant bookworm said, "I want to get married, have a good job and have babies." And she has done all those things. Cathy, the one with the fabulous voice who was funny, irreverent and made A's without trying said, "I want to become a famous singer and go to Hollywood." Today she is married to a producer, sings and lives in California. And I said, "I want to discover the secrets of the Universe. I want to find out the hidden mysteries of things." What prophetic words to have spoken over my own life!

This book, "Dialogues With The Angels", is the story of my personal quest to meet and interact with those Divine agents of God. It is the adventure story we have all dreamed of, and perhaps some of us have lived. Along the way, I have met devas, and masters, and beheld miracles. And finally I was destined, as many of you are, to meet my own beloved guides, who revealed themselves as the most powerful force in my life — even when I was unaware of it.

Since I was a child I have known such beings were near. But like many of us, I never spoke about this knowing to others. Now as I teach consciousness in cities around the world, many people come to tell me their spiritual tales; they are tales of healing, hope, miracles, and love. It is in the trust that this tale, the tale I share within the covers of this book, will find those kindred souls, that I now write it. It is finally time.

The Matter of Angels

Angels have long been a tricky subject. Invariably those with a more concrete approach to life consider that those who are interested in them just might be crazy. Some may even imagine that you have been struck with religious fever. This is not the case. Angels are beyond any religion, yet they can be found in almost every cultural and spiritual tradition of the world: Christian, Moslem, Jewish, Persian, Hindu, Buddhist, Native American, Greek, Roman, Mayan, Incan and Aborigine. Their stories go back to the earliest civilizations on our planet.

Some of our greatest thinkers have believed in them including Socrates, Plato, Paracelsus, Thomas Moore, William Blake, Milton, Shakespeare, Pythagoras, Homer, Jacob Boehme, and Emmanuel Swedenborg. St. Augustine once said that "every visible thing in this world is under the charge of an Angel." St. Thomas Aquinas wrote, "they are neither male nor female, but able to assume whatever form they like."

The human fascination with Angels has always been great, but perhaps never so great as it is today. Recent television polls tell us that 69 percent of the American public believes in the existence of Angels and another 67 percent in extra-terrestrials. Angels sites have surfaced on the Internet. Four magazines, and more than 140 stores in America alone now specialize in Angel paraphernalia. Films reflect this devotion, with movies like "It's a Wonderful Life" having become a Christmas classic. Popular musical songs include the word Angel in dozens of best selling tunes. Even television shows about Angels have found their way into the networks in the past two decades. Is this because more than 32 percent of the American public claims they have had first-hand encounters with Angels?[1] Perhaps. With these statistics, certainly even the most skeptical among us should consider that there may be some truth to these appearances after all!

Learning To Listen

Those people who do believe in Angels often discount their own experiences. We hear about Angelic encounters happening to others, without stopping to recognize the everyday miracles in our own lives. Because we are human and because we have doubt, we dismiss those "little coincidences" as insignificant, when in truth they are not. Angels take a million forms in a trillion guises. They speak to us in the movements of nature; through the appearance of animals, plants, and other humans; in the dance of the wind in the heavens; and especially in those little synchronicities of life.

Like many of you, I have wanted all my life to meet my Angels face to face. I have prayed, meditated, and called upon them in times of crisis. I have begged them to materialize, discoursed with them as invisible companions, and taken dictation at their hands. I have seen them appear at holy sites, I have heard them whisper in my ear, and I have seen the benediction of their presence over thousands. I have witnessed their appearance at the bedsides of friends' death transitions and watched them lift a spirit out of the body, leaving only the clay husk behind.

---

1 Life Magazine, *"In Search of Angels"*, George Howe Colt, *Time Warner*, (Dec. 1995); 65.

I am intimately acquainted with the Angels, and I feel blessed that my gifts of sight and hearing have allowed me to enter into the vision of the worlds they inhabit. To even begin to speak of the vast vistas to which they have taken me, is challenging at best. "Dialogues With The Angels" is but the first trail of bread crumbs leading down the path to their domain, but it will take you to the door of their open sanctuary.

Just what are the Angels - really? They are Divine helpers of Light and Love. Beyond that, the equation becomes much harder. To really understand the nature of the Angelic kingdom brings us to the very heart of understanding the nature of reality itself. And to do that, we must honestly come to terms with the fact that we live in a multi-dimensional Universe. This clashes with our current scientific model, which is only just now beginning to allow for such things as "near death experiences," out-of-body travel, and parallel universes.

No doubt, at this time in human history, when the veils between the worlds are once again growing thin, there are millions of silent ones experiencing the presence of these Divine teachers. This book is written for all of you. It is written to help affirm those inner knowings, those divine yearnings, and that part of us which feels a change coming to our planet. The time of Angels and humanity is coming once again, and we have lived to see it come.

I dedicate this book to all of you, and most of all to those beloved guides who have loved us for so long, and waited patiently for us to awaken from the sleep of our forgetting. May each of you come to have your own "Dialogues with the Angels."

Grace in Childhood

The Garden Angels

Like so many of us when we are young, I felt the presence of Angels from the beginning of my life. Yet the journey to come face to face with them seemed to take forever to unfold. And I was never good at patience.

As a child I often sensed them during the long walks I took in the north Georgia woods near my parents' suburban home. These invisible playmates called to me, rejoicing in the sounds of the crickets, the call of the whippoorwill, and the budding of new life springing from the richness of the forest floor. Try as I might, I could not quite see them except perhaps as a flicker of color or light out of the corner of my eye. When I looked directly at them, they seemed to disappear. I sensed them though, and I knew that they upheld me during all the painful years of my growing up.

When I was seven years old, I remember lying in the grass of our big front yard and looking up at the clouds. I used to imagine then that I could talk with the Angels. I would try to see the shapes of their wings in the wide, changing sweeps of cirrus clouds. I imagined that in the same way that I lay on the warm, moist hillside of our rich Earth, smelling the pungent grass through my nostrils, this vast panorama of clouds was their domain — an aerial landscape of immensity and promise from which they reclined to watch us on the planet below.

At such times I often felt like the oldest person on Earth. A sense of ancient knowing would creep over me. I felt that even though I was in the body of a child, I had lived many life times before and journeyed into this particular incarnation for a purpose. I did not know then what my life's work was to be, but I could feel around me all the sadness of humanity. I could sense, with the heart of an ancient one, the long centuries of travail the world has endured. I knew that in coming back to Earth, each of us makes a choice, each of us agrees to a task. But when we are born, the legends say, the Cavern Angel places his finger on our lips, causing our memories to be wiped clean. That is how we get the cleft in our upper lip. Then, the veils between this life and all that we have known in the heavenly kingdoms drops into place.

I asked myself, "Who was I really? What have I come back to do?" I knew as surely as I knew my name that every life has a purpose, but I could not bring back the memory of what my purpose was no matter how I tried. I used to listen to the silence of the great sound current roaring through my ears, wondering if it would tell me. Do you remember listening to this silence? Sometimes when you listen, there is nothing, no sound at all. Other times it is as if a deep, pulsing ocean roar lay beneath every other sound in the Universe, as powerful as the Cosmic Ocean itself, and as peaceful as a mother's whisper.

With any luck, the sound would help me to remember before I grew too old to forget. I could see that many grown-ups did not remember who they were anymore. They no longer listened to the roar of silence or the songs of grass growing through the Earth. They no longer believed in Angels' faces caught in cirrus clouds. They had closed the doors of their inner sight and hearing to such wonders.

I lived with innocence wrapped around me like the hug of a cloak on a cold, blustery night. My home life was far from perfect. My first memory at the age of three was of my father whipping me. My second memory, at the age of six, was of the same thing. But I trusted that Angelic Beings watched over all of us, even though I could not see them.

Did their wings not beat in the night wind when I knelt by my bed to pray? Did they not kiss me on the cheek when the breezes came through the curtains of my bedroom window late at night? Yes, the world was still a place of mystery, and magic lay like dew over everything I saw.

Many of us as children have this strong inner connectedness. Yet, as we move into the cognitive world of adult thought, we forget it. It is a sensing that lies beyond our intellects. It is the domain of our true spirits calling out to God. Christ once said that "except that we see as little children, we cannot enter the kingdom of Heaven." He spoke of the province of the heart, for true wisdom can only be known through the heart of innocence. It is only later, when we have donned our garments of self- critical adulthood, that we forget "the heart that would remember its name."

The Flower Devas

There were two places where I felt the Angels' presence around me most strongly, and I kept the knowledge of these places secret, as if knowing that the world of large tumultuous adults would not understand the sacredness I felt there. The first place was a flower garden. It was not ordinary, but a rich, vibrant well-tended feast of color adjacent to a neighbor's house.

I passed through it every day on my way home from school. The elderly couple who lived there were in the twilight of their lives. I knew instinctively that their children had left them long ago, so they poured out the last of their affection on the soil that abutted the wooded glade beside their house. Angels and devic spirits alike responded to the call. Lying belly down in the woods, I watched the couple several times, but I had no desire to meet them. They did not know there were Angels close, though I am sure they felt the comfort that the garden yielded up when they were in it.

I could feel the flower devas each time I ventured close. Two tall trees from the nearby forest formed an enchanted arch which led into the wonder of the blooms themselves. I could pass beneath those rich green limbs, like the arms of a waiting mother, to enter the place where angels sang invisibly from every bursting flower. Daffodils, day lilies, pansies, roses, gardenias, jonquils, and impatients all blossomed in a chorus of joy and sunlight. The flower devas danced in delight. They spun their magic webs in the glowing light of afternoon sun rays. I was enchanted.

After several weeks, I began to spend so much time there after school that my over-burdened mother grew worried. Where was I? Why wasn't I home when my two sisters were? One horrible day, she demanded to know why I was always late from school. What could I say? If I revealed my secret she would never understand. But I could not lie. Embarrassed and self-conscious, I told her of the garden. Then, like a prisoner forced to reveal the identity of her dearest friends, my mother made me take her to the place. Of the Angels, I said nothing. This one last secret I kept inside my breast.

The Broken Spell

We drove to the neighbor's house in a car. My mother straightened her dress and knocked on the front of the couple's house. The old woman came to the door.

"Hello," my mother began courteously, "I'm Carolyn McCannon. We live down the street. This is my daughter Tricia. I hope we're not intruding."

"No," the woman said curiously. "Is there something I can do for you?"

Patiently my mother explained that *her child* was visiting the woman's garden uninvited. She hoped I wasn't trespassing. Could we please come in? The screen door opened. We were brought into a dark, old-fashioned living room for tea that felt as if no one had lived in it for a hundred years. Lace doilies sat on old mahogany tables. Porcelain figures of small dogs lined the shelves. An old grandfather clock chimed in one corner.

I sat stiffly on a chair too large for me, legs dangling, face hot with anxiety. I didn't want to meet their scrutinizing eyes. What business did they have with me? All I cared about were Angels. I snuck peeks at the riot of flowers that lay beyond the sliding glass doors of her den. *There* was peace, I told myself. *There* the flowers waited for me to return and play. I hated this grown up dissection of things too sacred to be spoken.

My mother wanted to do the "right thing". The lady, she told me later, was a Baptist minister's wife. She asked permission for me to come and visit the garden again, and while it was a request of the greatest courtesy, in revealing my deepest secrets to a stranger, my mother did not realize she had betrayed my heart.

The old woman nodded, putting down her painted tea cup with a tight smile. "You may come in the afternoons," she said perfunctorily, "as long as we know you are here. My husband is away on Tuesdays and Thursdays, but I am usually home. If you are ever thirsty, you can knock on the door and we'll give you a glass of lemonade." She smiled at me, but our eyes did not meet. She did not know the secret of the Angels and I could not tell her.

I murmured a polite thank you, yet in that moment I knew that something precious had died. I would never return to the garden behind her house again. Its magic had been forever shattered. The gates which had led me to that first enchantment of Angels and woodland spirits had closed their doors to me, and I could not enter them again.

I prayed then that all the spirits who watched over me, the Angels that held my life in their hands, would lead me elsewhere. I hoped beyond hope that I would find another holy ground from which to meet them one on one. And this time I swore, I would never tell a single soul.

The Holy Spring

 second place of Angels was a magical discovery. It was adjacent to the huge woods that lay across the street from my parents' house. This was a large tract of land, perhaps a hundred wooded acres altogether. It ran between the street of our suburban house and the local grammar school, two miles away. Those were the years before the woods were taken apart, field by field, like the amputated organs of the Mother Earth herself, yielding to the surgery of suburban houses.

There was a creek close by. It ran through the woods behind our houses. It started on the wooded side, crossed beneath the road that separated it from our house and sped far, far down the road past the turn around of our dead-end street. This creek spread its fingers to gather trees, vines, bushes, and woods to itself, meandering far enough from the large backyards on the nicely built houses, that its pristine nature was a sanctuary for every adventurous child who cared to roam its forest.

The creek had been my playground from the time we moved there. It held the secret homes of squirrels and rabbits, snakes and possums, and occasionally a raccoon. I loved it totally. It was the jungle. It was our paradise. It was my home, even more than the bedroom I slept in. I climbed its trees in fall, waded in the shallow banks of its waters in spring, and captured fireflies every June night into the middle of the summer.

When I was eight years old I decided to cross the big road. It was a dangerous street and there had been many car accidents on it, so we were fiercely discouraged from crossing it. A large aqueduct connected the creek on one side to the mysterious woods to the spring on the other. It ran beneath the pavement, and its entrance was blocked by tangled vines. From my vantage point on one side of the road, I could see a direct path and an old sign that read "Elrod's Nursery".

Occasionally, an old man would appear beneath the sign, tending his plants from the haven of his ancient trailer house. I never saw any customers. Thin and wiry, the old man had a nose that ended in a bulbous knob. His skin was pock-marked and sagging. He wore a fisherman's cap and sometimes he carried a cane made from the saplings of the woods. He was an apparition guaranteed to frighten the most adventurous child of eight. Only the gleam of his blue-gray eyes beneath bushy brows gave any clue to the brilliance of his spirit.

I did not want anyone to know I was going there. I did not want the unfriendly eye of adults surveying this kingdom. One day I decided it was time. I crawled into the aqueduct and emerged on the other side of the road. If I followed the creek that ran through the aqueduct, I would be forced to pass the old man's trailer. He might see me. So I scrambled up the hillside into the woods above, paralleling the course of the stream until I was well past his trailer. Then I looked down and gasped. A grove of miniature standing stones stood in a circle beneath me. Beyond it was the source of the creek itself. It bubbled up into a pool of pristine waters. A little flagstone bridge ran across it. Perfect!

I ran down the hill. A quiver of excitement fluttered through me. This was a holy pool, cold and pure, which bubbled out the Earth herself. The old man had painstakingly cared for this place, building small bridges from bank to bank to let the creek flow without interruption. Rich thick moss encircled the creek and the small standing stones were arranged in a circle nearby. I gazed into the spring's mouth. There were four large goldfish swimming in it. I laughed aloud. This was a place of Angels and Devas. I knew it from the first moment I beheld it

The Elementals

Devas are nature spirits, usually invisible to the untrained human eye. They are part of the Angelic Kingdom and are in direct service to the nature world expressing themselves as Fire, Earth, Air and Water beings. They exist in the etheric world which penetrates our own, and they can be seen or felt with our inner senses.

They have been known in countless cultures and called by different names. To the Jews they were the Shedim. The Egyptians called them Afrites. Africans named them Yowahoos, Persians called them Devs, and the Greeks daimons. The classifications we have retained in our mythology are Greek. The Greeks called them Gnomes for Earth spirits (which means knowing ones), Sylphs for air spirits (those with gauzy wings), Undines for water spirits (creatures of the waves), and Salamanders for fire spirits (the Greek word for fireplace).

These nature spirits or Elementals, serve the Earth as part of the Angelic kingdom. They are the hidden energies which help plants bloom and which bring rainstorms in dry seasons. They can stand as small as children or twist into moving shapes of color. They appear and disappear to human sight in the blink of an eye. This is because they vibrate at a rate slightly higher than we do, so they remain virtually invisible to normal sight. Devas come in various shapes and colors, often taking on the visual characteristics of a particular area to match the mental picture imprinted in the human mind of those around at the time. They can usually only be glimpsed obliquely. They are most often seen in private places of lush vegetation. This holy spring was one of those magical spots.

Listening To the Devas

Many humans in other parts of the world, adult and children alike, have seen devas. Botanical experiments like Findhorn in England invoked these angelic cousins to help increase the growth of plants and vegetables in less than ideal soil conditions. Devas like harmony, and flee from areas of human conflict and stress. So if you wish to bring them into your garden, you must call to them from loving, meditative states. For someone just starting to tune into these shining beings, you may catch a fleeting color out of the periphery of one eye. When one looks directly at them, they often vanish.

Elementals are overseen by larger, Angelic beings who help them with their work. In that holy glade I was in the presence of both Angels and Devas, and I knew it. Most of us have sensed their warmth and feel renewed by it. Think how you feel when you come back from a day in the woods or a weekend at the ocean. The presence of these healing beings is part of the reason why. Our ancestors knew this well. At such moments we find that we are finally able to listen to the voices of our guides, to feel them reminding us of the Divine. And so it was with me.

I spent long hours staring into the depths of this ancient pool. I remembered other pools in other glades in lifetimes I saw as fleeting memories. And though my inner sight was only partly open, I could feel the Angels close, sense them all around me. I recognized this creek as an ancient spring, almost invisible to mortal men, but protected as a place of power by these Divine ones.

One day by the pool, I began to hear music. In the music was a poem. I got out my notebook and began to write it down.

My Secret World

My secret world in which I'm in,
All inhabit are my friend,
The oak and maple, birch and pine,
Are a few of the joys that are mine.
The leaves and grass, so tender and green
Are little of the things I've seen.
The tweeting voices of the birds,
Have sweeter song you ever heard?
The moss upon the rocks still stands
And trees still grow upon the land,
But will our children live to see,
My secret world, like you and me?

Even then, as a child, the foreshadowing of the changes that would come in our lifetime hovered over me. I knew with the instincts of a seer that the planet was being destroyed around me. I knew that the Angels who stand beyond time, who care take the beauty of this world and treasure each mountain and each stream, felt great sadness at the destruction we have brought upon the Earth. They grieved at the passage of any beauty, no matter how small, even though as long-lived beings they knew it was but a cycle in the endless wheel of time.

I told no one about this first poem except my mother. She alone suspected that something magical was happening to her child. Her own innate spiritual wisdom, hammered out in traditional Christian forms, sprang up again and again in her, sensing with that special gift of mothers everywhere that something of importance was being set in motion.

I began to receive poems regularly, pages of words that came into my head like a symphony. I could hear the actual musical notes, but I played no instrument. I did not have the musical language to translate what I heard, except into written words. The songs spoke of nature, the passage of time, the audible life-stream, of God, the indwelling of the Christ spirit, and the painful passage of humanity through all the lower worlds of existence.

I did not show them to anyone. I kept them to myself. I knew even then that to hear the Angels speak, one must be very still within one's self and reach out with more than the mind of adult possibility. One must be willing to enter the abode of the surrendered heart.

Walks With the Angel

 father had been raised Baptist. My mother was Methodist. My sisters and I attended the largest Baptist church in town until suddenly in my ninth year, as if by general consent, my mother began to search for a church that would answer more of our spiritual needs.

We tried several. I liked seeing the variety of ways God was worshipped. Even then, I felt there was only one Source and each Church had its gift to give. Furthermore, I did not think any of them had to be "wrong." The strangest thing to me was that they all seemed so fiercely attached to their own *version* of God. They were convinced that *they alone* knew God's plan for us, and through implied disapproval they judged the others. This seemed totally hypocritical when the essence of Christ's teachings was about embracing unconditional love. We finally settled on a gentle Episcopalian parish when I was eleven. It neither preached damnation nor made us feel guilty if we missed a Sunday. I was confirmed there at the age of thirteen. Today my family is still Christian, although each of my sisters has chosen her own interpretation of God's workings in her life.

There were three girls in my family, and my dad let it be known that he had wanted us all to be boys. He even named my younger sister Jon in the hopes that he could impart with his name, some of his patriarchal legacy. I tried to fill that role for him as athlete and scholar, and like so many other middle children, I saw my role as the peace maker in the family. I wanted all of us to get along. I wanted us to be happy, and I wished desperately that I could do something to make it so. Unfortunately, we rarely did. We fought as only the stubborn and strong willed can do.

I used to imagine we were large jungle cats thrown into one small cage together, trying to survive. "That which does not kill us, makes us stronger," became a silent motto in our household. If you can picture the speed of a Cheetah, the domination of a Lion, the power of a Tiger, the cunning of a Hyena, and the unpredictability of a Panther all packed into one small house, you might get a glimpse of my tumultuous family. We were joined in hardship and in pain, partners in a world of silent suffering.

A Shaman's Legacy

We were ruled by my father, one might say, the man with the iron hand. He was an ex-military officer and spared no words in meting out discipline. We were ordered to cut our own switches for beatings, and he frequently left us with blood on our legs and backs. His word was law, and to disobey meant punishment, clear and simple.

My father was *the* County Attorney, a serious title of serious consequence, since it was one of five counties of a major metropolitan city. He was the sun around which our young lives rotated. Like so many in our generation, my family was what we would now describe as dysfunctional, and I think we guessed it even then. Yet by the unwritten code of families everywhere, we kept our dark secrets to ourselves and did not tell a soul. This was especially true since my father was high up in the political community. We were told that his position kept food in our stomachs and a roof over our heads. To "tell" would cost the family its livelihood. Even now it is difficult for me to write about my family because of the invocation of silence that lies over all my childhood years.

My mother was the one we turned to in crisis, who gave us nurturance, creativity, artistic support and a glimpse of whatever happiness we had. She was a great woman, with a deep sense of loyalty and love, and no matter what difficulties my father impressed upon us, she was determined to stick it out.

My father was a man of considerable educational, political and athletic accomplishment. At the early age of 37 he had a massive stroke, and it had all but destroyed his life. Being from the John Wayne school where men flew planes, smoked cigarettes, drank Vodka, rode horses and expressed a limited range of fully charged emotions, his stroke devastated his life. It crushed his vision of his own manhood. In anger and pain, he began to take it out on us, making the long journey into alcohol addiction. Thus my sisters and I grew up in the dark, unhappy shadow of my father's repressed violence and bitter rage. And the fruit of it was far from sweet.

As painful as my childhood was, let me say that I have since noticed that many old souls have chosen similar dysfunctional family environments with the intent of learning particular lessons. Such pain forces us to look deep within ourselves and to seek for meaning in this puzzle we call life. One could argue that such an environment warps us. Yet, like the early Shamans who were often chosen because of facial or body deformations, the pain of such a situation produces its own type of powerful inner life. To escape the hell of external circumstances, we develop additional senses to our inner vision, our internal guidance system, and an attunement to God because that is all we have to rely upon.

Death Wish

At night I took long walks alone. I felt the pulsing need to get out of the house. Restless and frustrated, I called the wind as if she were my best friend. I prayed to the stars, that great reminder of

God's immensity, something we have lost living in our big cities. Sometimes I felt I could almost understand the language of birds and animals, just on the edge of knowing. Many of us have felt the magic of these things, if we but let ourselves remember.

I often sensed during these walks that I was being guarded. I reasoned that if the work I had come to Earth to do was important enough, then I could lie down in the middle of the road and Angels would lift me to safety if a car came. If not, my life would not be worth living anyway. I developed a death wish, knowing that nothing could be as painful as my life on Earth. To die would be to embrace a friend, to pass over into the world of no limitations and no pain. But I knew even then that it was wrong to kill oneself. To do so would mean that the soul must immediately return under less than ideal karmic conditions — and chances are one would only get something worse than what one had right now. No, that was not the answer.

Twice though, I lay down in the road, admonishing the Angels to protect me. Luckily, no cars came and my faith was not threatened by such an impertinent act. And who is to say there were not Angels watching over me?

Looking for Answers

When I was ten, I considered entering a nunnery, but a voice inside me spoke and said, "You have done that before. This time you are needed in the world." I considered being a doctor. I thought that brain surgery would be a wondrous thing, yet that same voice answered within me and said, "You have been a healer many times in the past. This time you are needed for other work."

I began to write and draw and I lost myself in books too numerous to name. At the age of twelve I came upon the "Razor's Edge," that wonderful book by Somerset Maugham. I thought that Larry's spiritual quest was the closest thing I had ever read to someone who knew how to ask the right questions. The suffering in my family demanded that I ask deeper questions of God. I wanted to know the true purpose behind all of this. If such acute emotional and mental suffering was allowed, there had to be a reason for it, and I wanted to know what it was.

In the days of the early 1970s, there were few metaphysical books around. If one wanted to study the hidden meaning behind things, the only books available were in traditional religious thought, philosophy, and a category called "the occult." Now occult actually means "that which is hidden," but in my family, it became synonymous with demonic. I was not encouraged to pursue that end.

The wealth of personal texts we now have on everything from meditation to visualization to natural healing, simply did not exist back then. It seemed that whenever I looked through any of the "occult" books of that time, the emphasis was on acquiring power, not wisdom, ego gratification, not love. That did not seem the right path either.

I knew there was something more profound that underlay everything, but I simply did not know how to find it. I began to pray each night by my bedside, asking for help from God, asking that the pain inside be eased. That was when the Angel first appeared.

The Angel Appears

I was twelve or thirteen, wrapped in the frustration of my family's internal wars, wanting a way out, not knowing how to find one. We had left my father several times, only to return to the prison of our home. There seemed no exit from the hellish cycle of alcohol, abuse, anger, tears and fear we had constructed for ourselves. To make it worse, we were forbidden any friends with whom to discuss our problems, since my mother could not take the chance that news of my father's problem would spread in the community. Frightened, estranged and trapped, my sisters and I stumbled through our teenage years.

My evening walks increased. During them I would often rant and rave aloud, feeling helpless to change my life or the lives of those I loved the most. Sometimes I thought I hated them. Sometimes I thought that if my father died all our problems would vanish. At other times, such pity rose into my chest that we would lose him that I was paralyzed with fear.

At such times I began to feel the presence of a powerful spiritual companion who walked beside me. I could sense him like an Angel of tranquillity. He strode beside me with a quiet power that belied my fearful heart and troubled spirit.

I would leave the house hurt and angry, pulling my jacket around me as the darkness of night moved in. I would rant and rave to the stars themselves, complaining about the injustice of my father's violence, my mother's frayed temper, my sisters' furious pleas for attention. Then I would hear as if inside my head, the deep voice of inner answers begin.

"Why does such suffering go on and on and on?" I raged in fury. "Why is it allowed in the world at all?" This night one of my sisters was in the hospital from an attempted suicide, another was suffering from an eating disorder. My mother was in the middle of a nervous breakdown, and I did not feel far behind.

"Suffering will end only when man is ready to let it end," he said within me. "Your father is not ready to stop his suffering."

"Well, I'm ready! Doesn't he see what his drinking is doing to everyone else?"

"Your father is in pain. He thinks that drinking will stop the pain."

"Well, I'm in pain too! And so is my mother and my sisters.

When does our pain get to stop?" Long silence as my words flung out at him.

"Perhaps if you let yourself feel a little of your father's pain, compassion would replace your anger. Then there will be less room in your heart for your intolerance."

'You're saying that if I have compassion for him, I'll feel love?"

"Yes, I am."

"And if I feel love, I can't be as angry with him?"

"Yes."

"Are you saying that love creates understanding?"

"Yes, it does."

"And if I understand him, you're saying I won't be as angry and frustrated with him, right?"

"That's exactly what I'm saying," the voice answered.

A long silence hung between us as I struggled with this way of thinking. I could almost hear his breathing as he walked beside me on the moonlit road. "Why didn't he just *materialize*?" If this Being was my friend, why didn't he just *show up* and put his arms around me? I wanted to be angry, even if it was at him. The hard knot of fury struggled to stay alive in my chest.

"All right," I finally said. "So he had a hard childhood. So his own father abandoned him. So the stroke took his physical strength and his sense of manhood ..." I could feel the edge of the knot starting to melt. "He's tired and sick and miserable .... He doesn't know any other way to be .... He thinks he's not good enough for us to love..."

The pain finally broke inside of me. That was it! ... not good enough ... I began to cry. "I just wish I could change these things ... I just wish I could help to give him back his life ..."

The presence of my Guide was palpable. "You can only change yourself, Beloved One. You can only change your own reactions to his pain."

I crumbled in grief on the dark curb, weeping. "It's too much for me to bear! If someone would just *help me* once in awhile ... but there's nobody ... nobody for me when I need it ...."

His strength fell over me like a blanket. But I was crying so hard I barely felt it. After a long time the tears became less. It was as if the Angel's invisible presence had put his hand upon my shoulder. "I am here beside you," he said gently. "I will not leave you now."

I wiped my cheeks and stood up. A strange peace enveloped me. I felt the kind of calm that comes only after utter despair. "Who are you?" I said aloud into the air. I could sense the luminosity of his presence, his tall body, but I could never see his face. "What are you called?"

"Does it matter? I am your friend. That is all you need to know for now."

"If you would just *materialize* ...!" I said into the darkness. "If you would just physically show up, I know you could make all my problems go away!"

"Your problems will be better when you, yourself are at peace," he answered evenly.

I pulled my coat around me in silence. I wrapped myself in the knowledge of his presence, telling myself that it was enough, telling myself that he did not have to materialize to make it better. His love and wisdom had been enough.

I mounted the stairs to our front porch. I could see the dark shadows of my parents through the windows. I took a deep breath and held it. Then I breathed out, watching it disappear into the frosty night air. I reentered the den of our trespass and sorrows. For a few hours at least, his love would bring me sanity and hope.

The Search Begins

Finding the Masters

 left for college when I was seventeen, and for the first time in my life, I felt I was free. It was a time of wild intensity and great expectations. It was a time when all of life was a great adventure, when we depart from the shores of all that we have known to chart our courses.

Usually at this time most of us experience a bit of battering that may take us by surprise, and then hopefully we begin to steer our course toward whatever stars we have set as our guides. Perhaps most difficult at this age is that many of us don't know what stars we have chosen, and thus the sea takes us willy-nilly into any of a thousand directions, and it is easy to get off course.

I was lucky. Because of my childhood I had a burning desire for truth which drove me, and it was this measuring stick against which I compared everything. After my first year in a small conservative southern college, I transferred to Florida State University in Tallahassee. And by the end of my sophomore year I had come under the tutelage of a group of spiritual masters called the *Vairagi*.

Vairagi in Sanskrit means "Truth," and this ancient elusive group of mystics rarely reveal themselves to man or woman. They are far older than they appear to human eyes, and only a handful have even retained physical bodies here on the Earth. Many have ascended to work with people on other planes of reality, meeting the seeker only when he or she can travel to the seeker's level of consciousness. Others will voluntarily enter the physical and astral domains of the aspiring student, and act as guides for inter-dimensional travel. The *Vairagi* Masters are adept at an ancient human science called Soul Travel — a skill each of us also possesses, that has been all but lost to the knowledge of modern civilization.

Looking back, I realize now that these Beings had watched me from a distance for many years before they decided to take me on as a student. Perhaps my prayers had been answered after all, but it took years before I knew it. Often it is this way with spiritual teachers. They will set up tests to be sure of the candidate's worth. What is most critical is whether the student perseveres in the earnestness of his or her intent.   It is also imperative that the seeker be living in integrity, for no true spiritual progress can ever be made if you are still lying to yourself.

Meeting the Masters

I happened upon these teachers because I had seen a poster on campus that read: "The Voice of the Master." It advertised a meeting on spiritual studies which was to take place one evening. I felt compelled to go. I had a film history class that night, so I arrived late and apparently the talk had ended. Students in the audience were asking questions, but the formal presentation was over.

I was immediately drawn to a chart at one corner of the stage. It showed the structure of the Universe with the many planes of Creation. "My God!" I thought. "It's a map to the inner worlds! At last someone can help me chart those places I have been going all these years!"

As if on cue, the voices and images around me faded. An intense white light appeared before my eyes. I could not see anything else. I heard a voice whisper, "This is the path I have placed you on, Beloved. Follow it."

It was the voice of the Angel who had walked beside me for so many years. Though I could not see anyone in the light, I could feel his invisible presence all around me. Then slowly, my vision re-turned. The room came back into focus and I could once again hear voices speaking in the hall.

"Can we study soul travel and still be Christians?" someone was asking the speaker.

"Of course you can!" I thought, bringing my attention fully back into the room. Several interested students were leaning forward in the front row of the auditorium. They were obviously intrigued but afraid to leave their Christian upbringings. The speaker shifted back and forth, uncertain what to say. I could see immediately in his auric field that he had not come to terms with his own Christian upbring-ing and wanted to throw the baby out with the bath water.

He opened his mouth to speak but couldn't think of a reply. I thought, "Tell them about Rudolph Steiner! Tell them about Saint Francis of Assisi and the Catholic nun Hildegard Von Bingen! Re-member Revelations? What do you think Saint John the Divine was up to?" But his mouth couldn't find those explanations, or perhaps he didn't know them.

I cleared my throat and stood up. "Excuse me, I think I can answer that question," I offered gently.

I explained then that the heart of the Christian teachings was acceptance for all of life, and that Jesus himself had said, "What I do, you too shall do, and more." He had also told them, "In my father's house are many mansions," referring to the many planes of heaven. Christ had performed countless miracles throughout his lifetime, which included not only "hands-on healing," but various forms of soul travel: These included seeing at a distance, materializing and rematerializing his etheric double, and remote healing. There was no contradiction between his teachings and our ability to prac-tice soul travel. In fact he had told us, "The Kingdom of Heaven is within." Soul Travel was an excellent way to start.

Afterward the speaker came up and thanked me for my comments. "How many years have you been studying with the *Vairagi*?" he asked curiously.

I smiled.

"Today. This is the first day I've ever heard of them, at least in the physical, but maybe they've been watching me from afar."

And it was true. Years later I was to hear many stories of people they had appeared to in Africa, Europe, America and the East, without having had any formal (outer plane) contact before. Many times it was years before they discovered that the master who had saved their lives, or had materialized by their bedsides, or had given them words of wisdom at a crucial point, was a member of the *Vairagi*.

The Dreaming Worlds

From that night on, my spiritual studies really began. These masters set up a program for me that was very intense. They taught me that Creation was composed of two primary forces: Light and Sound. This is spoken of in the Bible as "the Word." "In the beginning was the Word, and the Word was with God, and the Word was God." (John 1:1) This sound current, along with the Celestial Light, carries the vibrations of God throughout everything. The sound that I had listened to as a child was one of the expressions of the Divine that permeates everything.

The Vairagi then proceeded to give me direct experiences of God, not just on the physical plane, but on those we shall refer to as the Inner Planes. They showed me that soul travel is not only possible in the dream states, but that all of us can do it while we are still alive in the physical world.

Every night each of us travels in our dream state into other worlds of existence. For most people, since they do not know where they are going, or even that there is "anyplace to go," they never travel beyond the plane closest to the Earth. That plane is called the Astral Plane, and is the next vibrational rung up the ladder in the way that light and sound are mixed. On every plane of existence the laws of light and sound are operating, for they are the template upon which the Whole rests. But at each vibrational level, the laws of physics change. We perceive our world as fairly solid, yet as one learns to move into the higher realms, one discovers that this is not always so.

Most of us are familiar with the Astral realm because we have been there in our nightly voyages, so it is appropriate that I take a moment and talk about its sub-divisions. It is a rich and varied plane that stretches from the lowest low, to the illusion of clear Astral light which can be mistaken for the Godhead itself. It is not. It is only a reflection of that which lies above it.

Astral Levels

At the bottom level of the Astral Plane is the place of darkness. This is the cesspool from which all the negative entities spring. It is the place of the Hollywood horror movies. No one in his right mind would want to go there, and certainly no one would want to stay. This is as close to the Christian Hell as it gets. Nothing and no one stays there. Most of us have stumbled into this realm accidentally, sometime during the course of severe nightmares. The emotions which pull us there are greed, power, fear and control. If you can realize during your dream state that you are simply visiting, that this is not reality, then you can always get out while still asleep. Unfortunately, most of us are not that conscious, and we must "wake-up" in the physical world in order to shatter the spell of the dream itself.

The next levels of the Astral are the realms of creative imagination, where we externalize in what *appears* to be a manifested reality, those emotions that are the strongest in our lives. So emotions of hope, fear, desire and anxiety are often "out-pictured" in this reality. This is the type of dream where you are talking with your mother and she has your father's head. Usually, the images which are revealed in this type of dream experience, are incongruous with what we know of logical life. They are, in fact, symbolic of our emotions and the subconscious relationships our conscious minds have not yet formulated.

In truth, no one is present on that plane with us except ourselves, but the purpose of this plane is to provide a powerful mechanism for getting in touch *with what we feel*. It is the plane of hopes and dreams. For many people it is the primary place where their dreams occur. In this realm the subconscious can communicate through externalized "story scenarios" with the conscious mind, giving it hints and signals of danger, mayhem and desires we might be unconscious of. The operating principle in this realm is that if you get to play out those hopes and fears in the dream state, then it is not necessary to recreate them in your physical life.

Unfortunately since most of us don't allow ourselves to remember our dreams on a daily basis, we don't use this type of dreaming in the constructive way that it was intended. We forget these scenarios upon awakening. Thus we sabotage our subconscious mind's desire to communicate with us and dismiss them as mere fantasies.

At the higher levels of the Astral Plane we come upon real places of externalized reality. These are worlds where beings live. They may be souls we have loved before who have passed out of the domain of the physical world and are now living in a finer vibration. They may be cities of learning where teachers, masters and wise ones dwell. There are Universities at this level, villages, towns and a whole host of other cultures here. Exploring these worlds is fun and adventurous, and there are many opportunities to visit classes of higher learning and libraries of invention. I have spent vast amounts of time in these parts of the Astral, and these realms inevitably lead us to the higher paths where we may set our sights on more accelerated learning and growth.

In My Father's House Are Many Mansions

The Vairagi's teachings about spiritual law were vast and far reaching. Much of what I teach across the world today comes directly from years of work on these Inner Planes. I found through direct experience that Earth is one of billions of worlds in the physical world alone. In the higher realms there are even more. Planets are places where souls dwell to gain life experience. Some planets are vibrating at densities we can perceive, while others are more ethereal. Upon each world, those beings who inhabit it are in co-existent resonance with the planet itself. Whenever a discrepancy occurs between the planet and the primary life forms, something must change. This is what is happening on our Earth today.

We are certainly not the only dimensional reality that exists. There are, in fact, a total of twelve such planes, with twelve sub-octaves to each one. Seven of these planes represent those that we would see as manifested in the worlds of duality. This means that they were created for the express purpose of having light and dark, male and female, negative and positive as opposite ends of polarity. This opposition creates a certain tension, which we as souls agree to work within. This tension allows us to gain the experiences of discernment and choice. Exercising these tools teaches us everything from humility to courage, honesty to pain, servitude to self-actualization. And at the end of the day it teaches us love.

Throughout time these seven planes have been referred to in ancient literature as the "seven veils" or "seven heavens." The oldest mystic texts of many religions, including Jewish, Moslem, Hindu, Buddhist, Greek and Earth-based religions have also spoken of such levels. Since each of these planes is further divided into twelve sub-levels, we arrive at that classic number we have all heard about for ages, 144. As I was later to learn in the years ahead, numbers also express some aspect of Creation. 1+4+4 equals the number nine, and 9 itself is the number of completion.

From the point of view of travelers in the Universe, each sub-level of a plane appears to those visiting it as a separate vibrational plane altogether, complete with its own laws. It is only when one has reached the higher levels that one is able to perceive all of those below it. Thus, at our level of existence we have maintained the illusion that the citizens of Earth are alone in the Universe, even though there are many, many levels to Creation. And as our perspective shifts more dramatically in the years to come, the presence of these other beings, both Angelic and extra-terrestrial, will become much more pronounced.

Curriculum of Light

The kind of curriculum these Ascended Masters put me through was very intensive. This included years of nightly dream classes on higher levels of the Astral Plane and above, learning to repel negative entities at the lower levels of the third and fourth dimensions, and visiting museums and libraries not yet created on planet Earth. I met masters of great wisdom and learning. I learned to "fly" in my dreams. I learned telepathy and levitation. I met archetypal god-like deities in the fifth and sixth dimensions, and I sat in on councils who oversaw the running of our galactic quadrant.

I came to realize that everything that has ever been manifested down here on Earth has its beginnings in the worlds above. Thus the expression: "As above, so below," has many levels of meaning. Books that have not yet been written here exist in completed form there. Films that have not been made down here, can be viewed at the movie theaters there. Inventions not yet created on Earth exist in finished perfection there. That is how geniuses like Leonardo da Vinci were able to "bring back" from dreams the complex drawings of airplanes and helicopters more than five hundred years ago. His sketch books are full of inventions created on paper that our scientists have only now become sophisticated enough to understand in the last hundred years.

I also came to realize that the world we live in, that which we call the third density, is overseen by many benevolent beings who live in the fourth, fifth and sixth dimensional levels. They care about us, but they cannot make our decisions for us. We incarnated down here. They didn't. They can suggest, but they can't decide. As souls we became encased in bodies, and we forgot that there is anything outside of what we can experience with our five physical senses. In short, we do not remember that we are intelligent cosmic energy, indwelling the appearance of matter. And in that forgetting, we have lost all sense of who we are or where we came from.

We Have Lived Before

years into this intensive spiritual train-
ing program with the *Vairagi*, I found
that I was not only learning to remember who I was and how the Universe
worked, but I was starting to access information from the library of
the Akashic Records. For those of you not familiar with the Akashic,
it is the etheric memory imprint of all events that have ever happened throughout time. It is located on the Causal Plane, and the
records of all past lives are stored there. Well known psychiatrists
like Dr. Brian Weiss and Dr. Ian Stevenson, and hypnotherapists
Delores Cannon and Betty Binder have been researching this process of "remembering" who we are through hypnosis for decades.

As you may recall, I had the gift of remembering as a child, but
with little control over it. My parents tell me that between the ages of
eight and twelve I did, in fact, begin to speak fluently in foreign languages in my sleep. In answer to their perplexed bewilderment, I
had answered them, "Don't worry about it, mom. I'm sure I'm just
remembering some of my past lives and the languages I knew back
then." My mother had nodded her head worriedly, and kept silent.

As I progressed in my work with the Vairagi, I found my clairvoyance and clairaudience increasing. This caused me to ask a lot
of questions of my interdimensional teachers, and primary among
them was the mechanism of learning each of us as souls go through.
This brings us to the matter of reincarnation.

A Little History

Reincarnation is the belief that the soul, which is an eternal part of God, returns over and over through multiple lives to eventually learn the perfection of love for all things. For many people, Christ, Krishna and Buddha are symbols of such perfection. Reincarnation has been part of almost every major religion throughout history: Christian, Jewish, Buddhist, Hindu, Moslem, Mayan, Aborigine and Native American. In fact, unknown to many modern day Christians, reincarnation was fully accepted by Jesus and his disciples 2,000 years ago. It was integral to the mystical teachings of the Essenes in which Christ was raised and was included in all original Christian faiths.[1] That is why in the Bible there were statements like, "Is he Elijah come again?" They were referring to the prophecy that the soul who had incarnated as the great prophet Elijah in the Old Testament would return someday.

In traditional Judaism, reincarnation was considered one of the cornerstones of the Jewish faith until the mid 1800s when the urge to be accepted by the more "scientific communities" caused it to fade from public light.[2] Orthodox and Hasidic Jewish communities, however, still teach it today. In fact in psychiatrist Dr. Brian Weiss's book "Through Time Into Healing", he tells us that Rabbi, Moshe Chaim Luzzatto, author of "The Way of God", describes it this way, "A single soul can reincarnate a number of times in different bodies, and in this manner, it can rectify the damage done in previous incarnations. Similarly, it can also attain perfection that was not attained in its previous incarnations." Sadly, many raised in the Jewish faith no longer are aware that this teaching even existed in their faith.

---

[1] "Through Time Into Healing", *Dr. Brian Weiss, Simon and Schuster, (1992): 41.*
[2] *Ibid, page 40.*

Reincarnation and Christianity

Similarly, modern day Christians do not know the history of how reincarnation was removed from their faith more than fifteen hundred years ago. In 325 AD the Council of Nicea ousted reincarnation from official church teachings around the time of the Roman Emperor Constantine. Constantine was not having much luck controlling the growing number of Christians within his realm. Throwing them to the lions was not working. So he decided to legalize every religion. In that way, he could hedge his bets when he finally got to heaven. Constantine was a bit of an egomaniac, alternately proclaiming himself to be an incarnation of Zeus, Apollo, Ra, the Messiah and Jupiter.[3]

However, Constantine's wife did not want reincarnation included in these legalization processes. This third wife had risen as a notorious Roman prostitute to become the Empress herself. Constantine had "done away with" two other wives before marrying her, and they were a nefarious couple. Thus, when she insisted that if her husband was going to legalize the worship of all religions in Rome he should remove the teachings of reincarnation, he agreed. She didn't want to face the possibility that she might have to come back to Earth to pay for her evil crimes — and neither did he.

This suited the newly formed political college of Archbishops quite well. How could they hope to maintain control over a populace who believed they would have multiple chances to attain happiness or perfection? How could the teachings of an eternal Heaven or eternal Hell be enforced, if everyone knew that they were free to learn at their own pace? No. Control was definitely the way to go. So they outlawed these teachings and took most of the references

---

[3] "The Women's Encyclopedia of Myths and Secrets", *Barbara Walker, Harper and Row, (1983): 173-175.*

to reincarnation out of the literature of the Bible they were assembling.[4]

These all exist within the Vatican today. If you study the "Lost Books of the Bible," you will find other references to reincarnation. All quotes were not removed however, and any astute student can find them. For example, when Jesus healed a man who had been blind from birth he was asked the question, "Was this from the sins of the parents, or from the sins of the man himself?" Since the man was born blind as a baby, there was no way he could have sinned before hand, unless a belief in reincarnation existed in Jesus' time.

Many of the early church fathers, such as St. Jerome, Origen who was one of the early Church fathers, and Clement of Alexandria, strongly opposed this removal of truth and fought valiantly for more than eight hundred years for this suppression to end. By the sixth century, during the Second Council of Constantinople, the now "Holy" Roman Church had declared that teaching reincarnation was actually heresy.[5]

Yet this stubborn desire for truth was maintained secretly despite the threat of death. Reincarnation was taught in the hidden schools of the Knights Templar and the peaceful Cathar monks, though it was hidden from the everyday populace. Even as late as the 12th century, more than 50,000 Christian Cathars from Italy and southern France were exterminated by Papal decree because they knew about the immortality of the soul through reincarnation. That knowledge threatened the status quo. As Dr. Weiss has summed up so astutely, "the repression of past life teachings (throughout history) has been political, not spiritual."[6]

---

[4] *Op Cit, Weiss: 40.*
[5] *Op Cit, Barbara Walker: 847-849.*
[6] *Op Cit, Dr. Brian Weiss: 41.*

The Akashic Records

Throughout the centuries, many famous people have found that they could access information about the past (and sometimes the future) by looking at these Akashic Records. "Akashic" is taken from the Sanskrit word "akasa," meaning Spirit, since it is the etheric substance of the Universe itself that records these events. Some believe that the Angels are the record keepers and that this knowledge is stored in great volumes called the "Book of Life". People who peruse the Akashic will often describe going to a library where Angels attend them, helping them to find records of whatever is needed about a particular soul's journey. Some claim they see these unfolding images as a movie. This is how I experience them, unfurling like the tapestries of many movies connected by the thread of one person's soul vibration.

Christian mystics like Edgar Cayce, Rudoph Steiner, Madame Blavatsky, Emmanuel Swendenborg and Nostradamus all traveled to the Akashic library quite regularly. Some saw the future. Some saw the past. Others saw both. I see about forty percent future events. The rest are primarily concerned with the life patterns that a soul has formed up to the point when they come to see me. From these records I can determine the underlying issues and themes a person has grappled with throughout time. I can also trace the threads of well-loved relationships which have crisscrossed again and again. I am allowed to see and hear the Guardian Angels of the person in question, and trace energetic alignments from the Higher realms that lead us to find our own destinies.

Hundreds of thousands of people have undergone the direct experience of these types of things through past life therapy in the past fifty years. They have had their own direct knowing and even if their belief system did not previously include reincarnation, their world view shifted with such direct perception. Experience is not theoretical, as anyone who has fallen in love can tell you. What you see, hear, feel and have resonating within you is more than theory. Once you have had such profound realizations, no amount of religious dogma can dissuade you from inner knowing.

Over the Threshold

As a child I often saw past lives for others, yet the gift of "sight" came and went when it would. Sometimes when I would try to see something, I couldn't. Other times I would be flooded with information when I least expected it. Once I began to work with the Vairagi masters at the age of nineteen, I slowly steadied my inner vision, or "third eye" as the mystics have called it. And like any muscle when exercised enough, you cross the threshold from student to adept. So about ten years into my training, I crossed that line, which allowed me to begin to access information from the Akashic Records more easily. This enlarged view of the world gave me a doorway into seeing how totally original each of us is, and how our particular spiritual unfoldment has had a divine symmetry only a supreme Lord of Wisdom could orchestrate.

So ten years into my apprenticeship, an interesting change occurred. These dear ones who had so diligently worked with me for more than a decade, finally brought me to another group to study. This time it was an Angelic order. And thus it was that I began the next phase of my spiritual training which was to lead me to a whole new understanding of the celestial hierarchy.

Angels in New York City

first met the Angels in New York City, a curious place to see and hear Divine Beings, one must admit. Let me tell you how it happened. As a commercial photographer by profession, I had become deeply interested the year before in doing a photographic book on famous healers. So for a year or more, I had these very gifted healers coming to stay at my house in Atlanta, telling me the story of their lives. During that time I had seen incredible things — miraculous cures, laying on of hands, vibrational therapy, and crystal healing. The results were some amazing recoveries by those around me, who had seemingly incurable diseases.

I decided that it was finally time to go to New York to meet with publishers. I scheduled a flight to Manhattan, although I knew almost no one in the city. I had no idea who I was going to contact when I arrived, or even if they would see me. I had one friend who introduced me to some of his New York friends. This couple, Cannon and Brad, were very interested in consciousness and they invited me to stay with them.

For the first three days I attended a spiritual conference at a New York hotel, then moved to my friends' home. Cannon said on the day that I arrived, "Tricia, there's someone here I have a feeling you just have to meet. He's an Englishman, quite a bit older, but very much into Angels and healing just like you are. His name is Timothy Wyllie and he's written a book called "Dolphins, Extra-terrestrials, and Angels."

I said fine, I'd be glad to meet him and thus Timothy and I arranged to meet three days later.

Druids, Egypt and Drawings

We had lunch on the Monday following the seminar. We met in Central Park and strolled through the famous Strawberry Fields. The weather was stupendous. Spring was in bloom, and as we walked through the lush, green landscape of the park, I offered to do a past life reading for him.

Now Timothy is an extraordinary person, tall and almost emaciatedly thin, with a shocking mane of white hair. He is a bird person, and an ancient one at that. He even looks like a bird: high cheekbones, bright piercing eyes, a strong nose, and a graceful gait that belies his 6'2" height. He is an older man, maybe approaching sixty, but spry with the wisdom and joy of the spiritual exploration he has done for many years. I was pleased to meet him.

As we made our way through the park, I described lifetime after lifetime from his Akashic records which included Stonehenge and the Druids, Egypt and high priest work and other sites of ancient power. Quite intrigued with my reading, he invited me up to his penthouse apartment overlooking Central Park. There he lived with his small wren-like partner, Alma Daniels, in a bird's nest on the 27th floor. Alma is a psychiatrist, and has since gone on to write books on Angels.

I walked into the apartment and gasped. The living room was almost empty except for the large, ceiling-to-floor windows that swung out over the park. A beige colored pit-group inset itself into the wooden floor, giving the impression of open, clean space. It was the only thing that even indicated that humans, not birds, lived there.

"Would you like to see some of my drawings?" Timothy asked.

"Of course," I nodded.

He led me into a smaller room with a drawing table and desk. "Each of these take about five months to finish. They are each aspects of who I am." The first drawing he unfurled was of Stonehenge, complete with mystical symbols and Druidic patterns. The next was of Egypt. Each art piece was a direct reflection of the readings I had just done for him in the park.

He turned to me with fire burning in his sky blue eyes. "Now," he said warmly, "You see what a gift you have given me with your reading. Is there anything I can do for you in return?"

I thought about it carefully. "No," I said finally. "Thanks for asking, but I really can't think of anything."

"Well, what if we invite an Angel in to help you with your project?"

An Angel? Was he serious? Well ... okay. Of course an Angel would be very nice. I mean, if he could call in an Angel I would be *very* impressed.

"All right," I agreed, "I'm game. Let's call in an Angel."

The Angels Appear

Timothy lit a candle and we did an invocation for an Angel to show up. It was not very long, but it was very heart-felt. Then he embraced me in a hug. Suddenly, out of the blue, I heard as clearly as if someone were standing by my shoulder, a voice speaking.

"Asheena," the voice said. It was decidedly feminine. "Asheena." She spelled out her name, letter by letter. Before I could react, a second voice spoke. It was masculine.

"Beelub." He spelled it out, letter by letter, as if to be sure I would get it right.

"Oh my God!" I stammered, disengaging from our hug. "I can hear them speaking telepathically!" I turned my head and there they stood in the room with me.

Asheena was tall and majestically regal. She wore what appeared to be a Greek pleated skirt and top, sporting shin and arm plates and ready for battle. She carried a sword and a shield in her hands, and a magnificent strength emanated from all around her. I was speechless.

Beelub smiled at me. He had no armor, no weapons of any type. He was dressed in pale green pants and a slip over tunic, somewhat like the kind of dress that hospital workers use. He was a clean-shaven, rounded face Angel, slightly shorter than Asheena. No wings. He even seemed a little overweight.

I was stunned. This was not my idea of what an Angel would look like! He laughed aloud, hearing my thought. "I would rather tell a joke and lighten one's heart, than strike a sword," he said kindly. "It is much more economical, don't you agree?" He was a healer Angel, I realized, and had no need for weapons.

I struggled for words. "Timothy ... I can see them in the room. There are two of them here."

"Really?" He arched an English eyebrow at me. "Well, we shouldn't be surprised. I guess they have assigned themselves to you for this project. I'm sure you'll be in good hands from now on."

No truer words could have been spoken. I wound up getting to see wonderful people in the publishing industry and connecting with folks that I became friends with for many years. The Angels opened every doorway for me. Because of them, I made a resolution that when I returned home, I would create a holy space in which we could meet one on one, and I would get to know them better.

Angels, Altars and Voices

 had been thinking about creating a meditation space for some time. Having Angels show up in New York City simply inspired me to finally do it. I decided to put the altar in my bedroom since it was the only place in my house I knew I could be completely alone. For me, an angelic altar was a place from which to commune regularly with them. One can, of course, communicate with Angels anywhere. They are Beings whose very nature allows them to be present instantly whenever they are needed. But since I was courting a conscious relationship with these higher-dimensional Beings, creating such a sacred space from which to "be still" seemed a pre-requisite for accelerating my own spiritual growth.

Creating an Altar

I made it exceedingly simple. I put three white candles on a small, low table. I included a picture of Christ, a picture of an Angel, and some feathers. I didn't know why I picked hawk feathers at the time, although years later I would realize their true significance. I also had crystals, the clear quartz kind that transmit energy easily. I was just at the beginning stages of learning about the uses of crystals, which I learned we now use in computers, watches and satellites to conduct, store and transmit energy. I had begun to have detailed dreams about these crystal grid configurations, so I followed what my dreams told me to do in my meditation space, placing them carefully around me as I sat down.

On any altar it is respectful to represent all four natural elements of creation: fire, earth, air and water. The candles were fire, the fire of inner purification. Their white color represented the purity of my intent. The crystals represented earth, and I could have put an arrangement of flowers, leaves or even sand on my altar instead. The feather represented air. This is the domain of the winged ones, whether angelic or bird. They are the overseer energies of the land we walk upon. And lastly, water was represented by a beautiful shell that I had found at the beach.

You can add other things to your altar to help you to focus on attracting what you desire. I could have included pictures any spiritual teachers I wished. Devotees of Sai Baba and Yogananda, for example, claim much power from the beauty of their gazes. For me, I chose the holy mother, Mary, and a picture of Jesus. I also added a wall mural of Angels behind the altar itself. This reminded me of the connection I wanted to create. I might have also chosen representations of any animals with whom I had close associations, in keeping with Native American tradition. Many members of the animal kingdom are far more advanced than traditional western thought would have us believe.

If you create an altar for yourself, do it with love. Select only those things that are nearest and dearest to your heart. Clean it often. Replenish the fresh flowers, if you have any. Replace worn out candles or incense. Treat it with respect as *a living expression of your sincere desire to connect with such Divine presences.*

Phone Calls With Angels

I would pull up my floor cushions and light my candles when I first began. Often I would say prayers for anyone I thought needed support at the time — my friends, my family, myself or even other countries or world leaders. Then I would call in the white light of the

Christ energies, asking it to surround me in 360 directions on all dimensional levels. That way I had sanctified the space. I had created protection against any unwanted influences. Next, I would invite in my Guides and Angels. Even if I couldn't see them or hear them, the practice of consciously inviting them on a regular basis set up a bridge of communication which would eventually take on its own reality.

I came to look at this time as a two-way phone conversation. First I would do the talking, and then I would listen. Since my mind was often so busy when I began meditation that I couldn't be silent enough to hear them, I would speak aloud to them instead. I would say whatever was on my mind just exactly as if they were sitting in the room with me. After all, they probably were, and besides, they knew it anyway. Why should I try to hide from them? Besides, speaking aloud often helped me to clarify my real feelings and to lay out the issues that were troubling me.

Then, after I had said everything I could possibly think of, I would find that my mind would become still. I would finally be able to sit in the silence of myself. This is the time to listen, to listen for the answer to our prayers. So often I observe that we humans ask for help. We beg for guidance, but then we don't give ourselves the time to receive the very answers we have been praying for. Meditation is that time of receiving. It is a gift we give ourselves to "let in" the light of the heavenly kingdoms. It is the balancing to the constant chatter and giving out that consumes so much of our daily lives. And it is in that silence that miracles begin to happen.

Sometimes it would just have a sense of utter peace that would come over me. Sometimes lights would appear, glowing softly in my third eye. And sometimes the roar of the Cosmic Ocean itself would carry me away. There I would move into a place of no time and no space. I would often "awaken" from these sessions feeling that only five minutes had elapsed, yet the clock would say that it had been thirty minutes instead. I began to feel as if something profound was happening, even though my mind did not have the slightest idea what it was.

Healing Angels

Now because these two Angels had appeared in New York, I expected that they would follow me to Atlanta. I assumed that they were to be my personal guides forever. But I was wrong. I had wanted them to be my Angels because, after all, they were really amazing. I had particularly related to Asheena, for she was vibrationally aligned with the Athena archetype in Greek mythology. Queenly, wise, balanced and a warrior for Truth, I resonated with her energies. Yet I would never have imagined an Angel like her in a million years. But if there could be Angels like Michael, who stand beside God and holds the sword of truth before the onslaught of dark forces, then certainly there had to be Angels working with him on those front lines. Asheena was clearly one of these.

Beelub surprised me. His warmth and humor taught me the importance of picking the path of least resistance. Why fight when one can love? Why challenge when comradeship will do as well? He was an Angel who understood the principle behind all martial arts like Aikido and Tai Chi, letting the conflicts of daily life flow past us into harmony. His was the energy of a healer.

I expected that these two Angels would be permanently assigned to me, but after I left New York their presence faded. The healing project itself had come to a slow halt, although it had taught me an enormous amount about things beyond the average medical paradigm. I had seen incredible healers who had put their hands through people's bodies. I had seen crystals used to balance energy fields. I had seen colored lights used to cure cancer. I had witnessed "faith healing" from a retired Christian monk and heard speaking in tongues and laying on of hands. My perceptions of the Universe were permanently changed.

Finally I realized that these two Angels, Asheena and Beelub, had just come for this project alone. Once I was no longer focused on doing it, their work with me was finished. And so sadly I sat by my altar, hoping that some Angels somewhere would hear my call.

World Healing

It was then that I began to focus on healing in a different way. I began to pray not only for personal healing in my life and the lives of those I loved, but for world healing as well. This is an enormous task. It's just fine to ask that others be healed, but if we can't heal ourselves, our relationships, and our families, it's tough to take on all of Manhattan. Imagine taking on the world!

I am sure that the fact that I asked for this is one of the reasons that some ten years later I am now traveling, speaking and teaching. World healing is a tall order and it will take all of us working in small and large ways together to accomplish it. At that time in my life, I had a burning desire in my heart of hearts to help others, yet I had no idea of how to go about it. Looking back, I see it was no coincidence that it was then that I first began to hear the angelic voices.

Angelic Voices

Voices! Yes, I know it sounds strange, but that was exactly what happened: Voices like the kind we read about that Joan of Arc, Socrates, Carl Jung and Saint Francis of Assisi heard. Voices that spoke with melody and eloquence beyond my simple every-day expression. The voices would say things like, "God of gods, Lord of lords, deepest expression of Infinite Creation. We praise and glorify thee. We honor and cherish thee. We sing into Creation your worlds of being."

I was quite blown away by it all and even more stunned that they spoke in a language which, to my ears, sounded quite biblical. They spoke with "thees" and "thous" in the m   arnest praise of God Itself. This was the last thing that I had expected, and I was both frightened, amazed and in awe.

These sweet voices would begin while I was in meditation. I would find myself wanting to utter their praises aloud. But I was very self-conscious at the time, and although I was alone in my bedroom I could not bring myself to let them use my voice. I would look around the room, clear my throat repeatedly, and refuse to open my mouth. I simply could not let go of my own fears enough to allow those strange divine words through my lips, even though there was no human being around to hear me.

Within Christianity this is called "speaking in tongues" and can even take the form of speaking in strange languages that even the speaker does not know. Often there will be someone in the audience who understands the tongue, and thus the words will have great import to them. These words of praise cause a profound healing in those who are present, and I speak from my own experience of being healed in just this way that such a thing is possible.

Gifts of the Spirit

Speaking in tongues, prophesy and healing are considered some of the "gifts of the spirit" Christ told his disciples about when He said that men would do these things when the in-dwelling of the Holy Spirit came to rest upon them. I believe that any earnest heartfelt praise of God creates a vibrational harmony that aligns us with the wholeness of Intelligence God is. And it was with some real surprise that I discovered Angels themselves sing such constant words of adoration and love for God, words that praise the very Beingness we all spring from.

So this desire, which I was too afraid to allow into my world at the time, this desire for them to use my voice in praise of God, was the first step in my preparation to meet the Angels who were my guides. Yet I did not know it would be another five challenging years before they would present themselves to me face to face!

The Greek Oracle Temple

 few months after the voices first began I had a most unusual dream. It was a lucid one with a *Vairagi* teacher I had been working with. I had been going to temples, museums and libraries on the Inner Planes for years, yet this trip was different. We were visiting a Greek Oracle Temple on the Astral Plane with the intent of hearing the Oracle speak. I had never been to a Greek Temple before, let alone one like the Oracle at Delphi.

Looking back, I realize now that this was a set-up. Since I was so afraid of allowing the Angels to speak through me in the waking state, my teachers had found another way to let me experience "channeling" in a most profound and direct manner. I remember the event as if it happened yesterday.

We found ourselves, the Master and I, traveling up two escalator flights of stairs. This is usually indicative of the number of planes you are moving through. My teacher, a striking fifth dimensional poet named Rumi, led me into the courtyard of a beautiful building of rose quartz. It was a classic temple with eight fluted Doric columns upholding a pointed roof with a dome on top of it. A patina of white and rose alabaster shells created a large courtyard in front of the steps coming down from the columns. When we arrived, the steps were empty as was most of the courtyard.

Rumi was dressed in a blue, belted tunic that seemed to fit in effortlessly with the time period itself. His dark curly hair framed a bearded face and deeply penetrating eyes.

"Where are we?" I asked in wonder.

He looked at me kindly and smiled. "We are at the Temple of a

Greek Oracle. This temple is similar to the ones used on Earth during the time of your Greco-Roman culture."

"Oh, great!" I said enthusiastically. "I've never heard an Oracle speak before!" In fact, the truth was that I had never even heard a medium or a channel speak. "When will he come out?"

My teacher shook his head. "The person who would channel this entity is not here. In fact, there are only three or four people on this planet capable of handling this entity's particular vibrational pattern."

"Oh ... why is that?"

"In order for someone to be a healthy conduit for a particular consciousness, they must first come into sympathetic alignment with that being's vibrational patterns. Thus a link is formed for communication. Without that, one cannot be an oracle."

"Well .... fine," I said enthusiastically. "Any one of those four will do. Bring them on."

Rumi hid a smile behind his hand as he stroked his beard. "I see you don't understand me yet. None of those people are here right now."

What?! I could not believe my ears. "You mean, we've come all this way and there's no one here to channel this being for us?" This made no sense at all! It was like going to Disney Land only to find out it was closed for the holidays.

"That's right," Rumi nodded with a twinkle in his eye. "None of them are here at the moment."

Now perhaps if I had reflected on it, I might have seen where this was leading, but all I knew at the time was that I wanted to hear the Oracle speak and it seemed a shame to waste the trip.

"Well, could I try?" I asked curiously.

"Of course," Rumi bowed. "Be my guest."

And that is how it began. I sat down on the square at the top of the temple's steps and closed my eyes. I distinctly remember that the rectangular stone was a pale pink marble. It was cold to the touch. The columns stood just behind me and to the right. The steps were below leading to the courtyard. No one was there, except for a couple of miscellaneous visitors and my teacher.

My first attempt was pitiful. "I don't understand what I'm supposed to do," I complained, hoping that I didn't sound like I was whining.

Laughing softly, the Master explained how it was done. "Clear your mind and begin to breathe. Ask the Being who speaks in this place to speak through you. Let yourself melt away. Just surrender."

Suddenly, as if it were completely effortless, I felt an energy come in through the top of my head and seat itself in my throat. It was very sudden and *very real*. I jutted my chin forward as the energy settled into my voice box. My mouth just opened. Words came out — words that were a deeper octave than my normal voice. And what was even more incredible was that I had no idea what the voice was going to say until my ears heard it!

The sensation was like nothing I had ever felt before. I cannot adequately describe it. It was much stranger than listening to another person speak. I had never thought about it, but often in conversation with someone else we can actually intuit what they are about to say. But with this experience, I had no idea — I mean NO IDEA — what the voice was going to say, and it was my voice speaking! It was as if the words were not even being run through my mind at all!

After a time, I began to be aware that a small crowd was gathering for the Oracle. They were asking questions of him, or rather of me with his consciousness. I found myself wondering if I could "see" what it was that I was going to say before it came out of my mouth.

And at that point things began to change.

I started seeing images. The sound of the Oracle's voice grew faint and distant, as if somehow "I" (my consciousness) had moved away from my body. I followed the flow of these images as the Oracle spoke on. I seemed to be in a place where time operated differently. Much time was passing in the Temple, yet I was suspended beyond it all.

After awhile I became aware that someone in the crowd had asked a question about the discovery of a sunken treasure that had gone down with a ship. The images of where that treasure were sped by me, and I knew the voice was telling them. But I didn't care. I remember thinking to myself, "I'm not interested in this. This is boring for me. There's nothing for me to do here. I don't care about this sunken treasure." And with that, I decided I wanted my body back.

Suddenly I was distinctly aware of another reality —that of being in bed at home on Earth, the reality of my third dimensional human world. Simultaneously I felt myself sitting up in bed, and I sensed that it was morning. Furthermore, I heard myself speaking aloud. I realized then that the Oracle's voice was still coming out of my mouth as I was reentering. I was channeling on both the physical and astral planes at once! Holy cow!

Creating a Vow That Would Change My Life

Now this shook me up quite a bit. Not only did it seem to be a major breakthrough in my ability to be a conduit for spiritual information, but I was not at all sure I was ready for it! I was excited and I was scared. I honestly didn't know what to think. I realized that I had done this work many times in the past, as healer, oracle, priestess, priest, and seer, and in some of those life times I had been killed for it. Now here I was again, and the idea terrified me.

For those of you reading this, these things may sound exciting. Perhaps as a story, yes, but this was my life. And you must remember that although I had heard and seen extraordinary things my whole life, I was raised in a conservative Christian family. Channeling was considered highly suspect. After all, demons could be anywhere, lurking in anything. For centuries we have been taught that anything mystical or other worldly could be a deliberate ploy of Satan's to mislead the faithful. These beliefs were etched into my consciousness from years of early training. Now I had done it. I had stepped over the edge. Had I gone too far? I didn't know.

My heart told me that this Oracle was a benevolent being, and I trusted my teachers completely. I had been under the constant supervision of the *Vairagi* the whole time. But, I decided, I simply did not like being "out of control." I didn't like being "gone" from my body while the whole thing was happening. I liked *knowing* what was happening to me. I wanted to be present. I didn't just want to be a disinterested bystander.

I decided then and there that if I was going to channel, I wanted to be a conscious part of what was happening. I wanted to be right there learning along with everyone else. And I didn't want to just give messages about psychic things like sunken treasures and romances. If I was going to do this work, I would only work with an energy from the Angelic realms that would uplift those around me into a state of greater peace and love.

Because of this decision, which I believe my Masters approved of, it was to be many years before I was given the opportunity again to channel. In those five long years of waiting, I longed terribly to meet my guides. Yet I knew I was being prepared for what was to come, and I was constantly reminded that "you can't push the river."

The Angels I had begun to work with did a lot to help me process my deep fear and surrender issues to make that meeting possible. They knew that I could not get my wish fulfilled until I had raised my own Light to a point where I could handle such celestial contact. And they were right. In essence, I traded the "short-term" experience of just working with a fourth or fifth dimensional entity for the "long-term" hope that I would one day be clear enough to dialogue with the highest of the high. And to do this, I had to let go of a lot. I had to release my personal attachment to getting somewhere quickly. After all, I asked myself, where was there to go?

Most of all, I had to let go of my egoic nature. And this act of "letting go" is perhaps the most difficult aspect of growing spiritually that we can ever do. It is the one thing that all of us must ultimately address in our paths to enlightenment. Surrendering to God, surrendering to Angels or even to communication with our Higher Selves is like peeling away the onion layers of our own little Egos. It is difficult and it is constant. It is the work of Eternity.

Some say such enlightenment happened to the Buddha in an instant, but we often forget that it took an entire life time of preparation for him to make that final jump into the abyss. Let us each remember that this is what we are doing with every moment of our lives — preparing for that instant when we too shall jump from the mountain and grow wings.

Tools For Transformation

Before we continue our adventure tale, it is imperative to take a moment and consider what lies behind these years of training. And also to weigh how each of you may learn to open these dormant spiritual abilities for yourselves.

Currently, scientists tell us that we humans use somewhere between 7 percent to 10 percent of our brain capacity. If this is true, then we must ask ourselves, just what is the other 90 percent created to do? My guides have said that each of us has within our neural circuitry the ability to access that "great galactic computer in the sky." In other words, inherent within our physical and neurological makeup is the potential for going "on line" with the Divine knowing of the entire Universe. Just how do we awaken these inner gifts? How do we connect this circuitry so that we access more of our innate wisdom?

There are many ways to do this. In this chapter we will be discussing several. For a moment though, let's just imagine what our world might be like if we really used another 10 percent of our brains. We might all find ourselves becoming *very telepathic*. Then it would be difficult to live in a world of deception, whether in politics, media, relationships or even consumerism. We would *know* when someone was lying. How completely wonderful!

What else might we do with that added brain power? We might find ourselves healing one another's illnesses, or even extending our own lifetimes because of our ability to rejuvenate our cells. We might discover that we could stay in touch with loved ones at a distance, monitoring their safety or their progress, dropping in upon them like a telepathic phone call. How completely marvelous!

Acknowledging the Inner

Unfortunately, most of us were taught as children to ignore these natural abilities. Their existence was not even talked about. So like any muscle, they began to atrophy as we became adults. If visionary dreams of danger came as a child, your parents probably told you to go back to sleep. "It's only a nightmare," they said. Yet in our dream states, we have access to the Inner Planes in a way that our normal beta brain waves do not allow. We move into advanced states of Theta and Delta, from which great information can be gleaned.

So the first step is to become aware that we even have these extra-sensory gifts. It is to acknowledge that it is a natural condition for human beings to be able to trust their intuition, and to ask for inner guidance from the Universe directly. How often has each of us ignored his or her own inner knowing, and lived to regret it? Many times our "gut response" nudges us to consider knowledge that is not readily available to our logical minds, yet upon retrospect we realize that those responses had a clear wisdom behind them.

What other things might have happened to you that were dismissed by your "rational" mind? We often dismiss the synchronicity of people, places and things, forgetting to thank the Universe for our unexpected boon, forgetting that this is how Angels most often work. How often has the very thing that we most needed in the moment shown up unexpectedly? And have we stopped to practice an "attitude of gratitude" in thanking God for these blessings?

Our intuition is a direct line to our Guides and thus to God.

How often have you trusted your intuitive inner voice, and found that everything turned out just fine? Think about the little ways that this shows up in your life. How many times have you known who was calling when the phone rang? How often do you "guess" which line is moving faster at the automated bank teller? How many times have you had a feeling that things were not right with someone at work and later discovered your "hunches" were correct? These are all ways that your brain is picking up on data available in the Universal current which has gone virtually unnoticed by your conscious mind, yet is filtering through to aid you in your life. With only a little attention and practice, this alignment with the Universal current can be increased ten-fold.

Creative Visualization

Creative Visualization is one of the greatest tools for learning to connect your Beta brain, or normal waking state, with an Alpha state of consciousness. When we dream at night, we dream in Theta and Delta. Often times we awaken quite suddenly and lose all memory of what has occurred during our normal dreaming cycle. Dreaming is a doorway into the Universal current because during sleep our brain waves enter states of awareness which are beyond that 7 to 10 percent figure. We tap into circuits that our waking state does not know how to enter. Alpha is the brain wave state that lies between the two worlds of waking and dreaming. It is the bridge state where one remembers how to move into the higher realms of consciousness.

Creative visualization is the conscious mind's practice of using thought to create manifestation in this dimension. One can use creative visualization to contact the Universal current and request a specific outcome. This may relate to any matter of creation. It could relate to a job, a relationship, even a weight problem. By specifically focusing on that which you wish to create, and seeing it done, the forces which will support its manifestation begin to be attracted to you.

This is but one type of tool for helping to create your reality. But in order to use even this one successfully, a little homework must be done on the human personality to clear the communication wires between you and the Galactic Computer.

Opening the Channels

First we must deliberately align our conscious minds with the Universal current and surrender to the highest form of what we are. This doesn't mean that we can't request something specific. Of course we can! But perhaps God has a higher plan in mind for us, and it is far greater than anything we could have thought of on our own. So you always want to use your prayers to leave a space for the unexpected to happen. I often pray in such a way that I say, "I would like to manifest this, or something better for me. I release all my desires to the Universal abundance, knowing they will be fulfilled." It is amazing how well it works!

Secondly, as human beings we must be willing to clear out those aspects of our subconscious which need to be healed. The Higher Self operates through our subconscious minds. Few of us are really clear enough to hear it on a daily basis, except through the nudges of the subconscious. And if our subconscious is clogged with years of emotional debris, it becomes difficult to get the transmissions clearly.

To continue our computer analogy, let's imagine that the "on-line" hook up can only occur through the subconscious self. Most of us think that in order to get the attention of our Higher power we have but to pray, or to wish it into existence. In truth, our Angels are always with us. We already have their attention, and yes, the conscious mind is very important in focusing your will toward a conscious relationship with God. That is the true power of prayer. However, these communication channels with the Higher Mind come through the subconscious network. That is why ancient prophets of old often experienced God through their dreams. During our dream state, we too are in the brain wave states of the subconscious mind, and thus the Higher mind can communicate with us more easily.

Clearing the Filters

Because I had paid attention to these subconscious states of consciousness and deliberately developed an acknowledgment of my inner sight and inner hearing, unlike many of you who also came in with these neural circuits open, mine did not close down. Mine remained open, with the communications lines in tact. Still, the very act of living on a planet which is so archaic in its spiritual and social perspectives produces emotional debris in all but the most advanced of avatars. These conflicting emotional messages take a thousand forms. They are insidious and wide spread and sound like dozens of euphemisms you have been told directly or indirectly.

You aren't good enough, and you never will be.
You must be perfect to be Loved.
You were born in original sin, so you are damned before you start.
Your God given sexuality is bad.
If you are a girl you must be a whore or a virgin.
If you are a man you aren't allowed to cry.
Your innate spiritual curiosity and abilities will lead you to hell.
Money is the ultimate God.
You can't trust the ones you love.
Animals don't have feelings, so it is all right to kill them.

You get the point. These messages are amplified in many ways. The media, our churches, our school systems and our peer groups reflect these things to us because they have received the same conditioning that we have. And because we are given unhealthy signals about who we are and who everyone else is, we get static on our receiving lines. These limited human belief systems clog our filters. Stumbling through such confusion, is it any wonder that our emotional lives are often in such turmoil?

When these unresolved fears and emotional issues from our past block the channels within, we cannot really tune into the inner realms very clearly. Therefore we must find a way to dissolve these emotional blocks if we want to get on-line with the Universe in any conscious way. And just how is this possible? What do we need to do to get ourselves on track? This brings us to the work of inner healing.

New Paradigms

There are many ways to approach this healing process, and there are as many paths as there are people on the planet. I have found that at the beginning of any spiritual awakening process our celestial guardians are at our elbows, steering us toward the tools which will most help us. So trust this process first. Trust your own innate responses, and then let yourself be led.

It may be that you are led to read a special book, like this one, or to attend a lecture or a seminar. You find yourself wanting to reexamine your spirituality or even to get more involved with your Church or synagogue. You may go to a metaphysical event, or one of those powerful 12 step programs . You may find yourself wanting to connect to "a Source Higher than yourself" in a non-denominational way. You may try meditation, yoga or Tai Chi. You may join a men's or women's support group. You may take a class — or even teach one.

At such times you should remember that old spiritual maxim "We teach what we most need to learn." It is how we practice our own self-mastery.

In pursuing self-healing you might also want to look at the changes occurring in therapeutic psychology. During the last twenty years some powerful new techniques have merged from this arena, including transactional analysis and voice dialogue, both wonderful ways of getting in touch with the many complex parts of ourselves.

Self-empowerment seminars and relationship training allow us to gain new perspectives on old ways of doing things, from relationships to careers. Rebirthing techniques and cellular massage are two of the most powerful ways I know to release pain while bypassing the mental body. Both of these tap into the very core of any pain which is trapped in the physical or emotional body when such trauma occurs. I recommend them both.

Hypnosis is another incredible tool for moving into "non-ordinary" states of consciousness to access events which have affected our subconscious deeply. This is not only true of traumas in this lifetime, but in others. Some astounding work has been done with this kind of past life therapy by brilliant pioneers like psychiatrist Dr. Brian Weiss who wrote "Many Lives, Many Masters" and "Through Time Into Healing." These two books alone have greatly contributed to changing traditional approaches to psychology in the last twenty years.

Getting Lighter

Whatever ways you personally use to expand your own human belief systems and cut through the baggage of emotional static, remember that you are doing so to make your life better. You are dislodging years of emotional conditioning that is cleaning the static off of the lines of communication between yourself and the Divine. Merely the willingness to be deeply honest with yourself is enough to begin this releasing process. It is the first step you take upon the journey to self-discovery. When you are willing to confront your deepest fears and trace them back to the belief systems that created them, you will find that problems that have plagued you all of your life will disappear forever.

All the knowledge in the world will not help to enlighten you, if you don't allow yourself to become lighter. The more each of us lets go of his or her unconscious, unprocessed emotions, the easier it is for us to embrace the gifts of inner knowing that we have cultivated over life times. Thus our lives in the here and now begin to flow with more joy, more ease and more abundance.

Healing With the Angels

 was Autumn. The rich tapestry of colors that make up the Great Smoky Mountain Parkway was flourishing all around us. Flame red, green, gold, orange and brown, were brilliant and calling. I was restless. One Friday afternoon, at work, the phone rang. I picked it up.

"Hi Trish, this is Gail. How are you?"

"Hey, Gail!" I said. "It's great to hear from you." Gail worked at a local ad agency as a traffic control manager on major advertising projects. She was a smart, pretty, dark-haired woman with a great figure, a bright wit and a tomboy charm. We had been friends for two or three years and had the pleasure of working on a couple of advertising jobs together.

"I've got the itch to go camping," she announced. "My boyfriend's away for the weekend and I thought ... well, maybe you and I could pack a picnic and drive up to the Smoky Mountain Parkway tomorrow morning."

"I'd love it!" I shouted. It was just what I needed. "Your house is 45 minutes north of town, isn't it?" I said. "I'll drive up at 10:00 a.m. and pick you up. We can go from there." She chatted a little longer and then we hung up. Little did I suspect that this was the beginning of an Angelic encounter that would change both of our lives forever.

The next morning Gail rang me before 9:00. She was crying on the phone. I could barely understand her words. "I've ... I've called an ambulance. I'm burned. I ... I think I've done something serious to myself."

"What?" I could not imagine what she was talking about.

"I ... I spilled a pot of boiling water all over my arms," she cried. "When the skin slid off and fell onto my leg ... I ... I think I'm in trouble."

"Okay, tell me what hospital. I'm on my way." I grabbed my purse and jumped into the car. By the time I got there she was in critical care with the doctors. Finally one of them came out to see me. He looked worried and gray.

"Your girlfriend has had a terrible shock. She has second and third degree burns all over her arms, from her wrists to her elbows. Furthermore the water severely burned her left foot. It took the skin entirely off. We could see exposed bone and muscle when she first came in."

"Oh my God! What can I do?" I cried.

"You can call her parents. Tell them to come down. She's going to need some round the clock care for awhile."

"How long?" I said.

He shook his head. "She won't be able to function for many weeks, I'm afraid. I'm sorry. You can go get her prescriptions filled. We've given her the strongest thing we have for pain, but I'm not sure what good it will do."

I was numb as I walked into the pharmacy. At the nurses station I called her parents, relaying the doctor's messages. They agreed to drive down from North Carolina within the hour. "I think you'll be staying for awhile," I said as steadily as I could. "It looks pretty bad." Her mother thanked me profusely and rang off. They were there within three hours.

The next day I drove over to her house to see her. Her kind, pretty mother greeted me at the door. She was a sweet woman, but worry stood in her gray eyes. "She's trying to sleep," she said softly, "but the pain's so great she just lays there and cries. I don't know what to do."

I went into the bedroom. It was dusky and shrouded. I couldn't think what I could possibly do to help. Gail managed to greet me with a joke. "Hey, why didn't you bring your camera. I look like a mummy in all these bandages."

It was true. Her two arms were wrapped in thick gauze. So was her left foot all the way up to her knee. She tried to laugh, but she started crying.

I sat down stricken. "Oh Gail, how can I help?"

When she could find her voice again, she tried to make a joke. "Well, this is the time to invite in some of those Angels you talk about so much. I wish some of that metaphysical mumbo-jumbo stuff really worked."

Brilliant! I stood up. The beginnings of an idea had just crested in my mind. "Okay Gail ... let's do it. If you're willing to let go of some of that pain, I think maybe I can help."

Her mother handed her a tissue and she blew her nose. She tried to make her comeback light. "I'll try anything once." Her voice broke on the last word.

I fought back my own tears and stood up. I would need a certain clarity and detachment to do this correctly. I told her to close her eyes, and I called in the White Light of Spirit. I prayed silently to my Angels for help. I knew that this was larger than anything I had ever attempted.

I asked Gail to start breathing in deep, slow waves. "Imagine that with every breath you take, you are inhaling a color," I said. "The color is a soothing green. Green like the damp, cool color of forest leaves. With every breath, pull the green color into the top of your head, and feel it go down into your chest, filling and expanding your lungs. Now feel it run down your shoulders and arms, taking the burns and pains with it, out towards your fingertips."

In a thirty minute session of pranic breathing, I gave her suggestions that every breath would cleanse and regenerate her body. All the pain and debris would be pushed out of her fingertips and out the bottom of her feet. We went through a sequence of colors, and I programmed her subconscious mind over the next few days to continue this cleansing whenever she breathed.

When I was done, Gail was sleeping soundly. Her mother helped me to the door. "This is the first time she's slept since it happened. Thank you so much."

I shook my head. "We should thank the Angels. They're the ones who do the work." I hugged her hard. "I'll try to come back sometime this week."

The Miracle of the Angel

It took me seven days before I returned however, and this time I brought with me a wonderful friend named Helena. Helena was a sixty-five year old woman who worked with Angels. She had pictures of them in her house, statues of them in her bedroom, and she drew Angel cards every morning before breakfast. I thought that if anyone could help me with Gail, it would be Helena.

When we went into Gail's room she was sitting up. She smiled wearily at us, trying to be cheerful. "Thank you for the other night," she started. "The drugs weren't even touching the pain. Maybe there's something real to all this weird stuff you talk about. I know it sure made me feel better."

Helena and I smiled. I introduced them. "If you want us to, we're going to do another session with you."

"Hey, I'm game. I couldn't feel any worse. My job just called. They're firing me. They said I'm going to be out too long. The doctor says I'm gonna have scars, and I think I've just decided I hate my life." She shrugged. "Do anything you want with me."

Helena kissed her forehead. "We'll take care of you," she said motherly. "I'll call in some Angels."

As we had done before, I had Gail close her eyes. I began making passes over her body, just as I had done the previous time. I spoke slowly, having her draw her breath in long deep color rays that penetrated her whole body. Helena stood on the other side of the bed praying. After many minutes of this I felt the time was coming to bring it to a close. I looked down at the end of the bed, directing her to push the pain out of the bottom of her feet, and there for the first time, I saw an Angel.

She was very tall. She had long dark hair and she wore a deep purple gown. A bright radiance shone all about her. My mouth dropped open. All of her devout attention was focused on Gail as she lay, eyes closed on the bed. She smiled slightly and looked up at me as if to say, "All is well. I am here." I felt a wave of love entering my heart, and I began to describe aloud what I was seeing to Helena and Gail. But before I could speak more than a few words, I felt the presence of the Angel come around the bed and slip into my throat. She began to speak to Gail with my vocal cords.

"Do you not know our Beloved Gail, that we are all here with you. Through all your hardships and travails, we have always been here. Long has your journey been and it is known to us how often times you have suffered, even at your own hands. Come. We offer healing. We offer love. We offer succor. Remember to love yourself most of all. Know the breath of our Spirit is upon you. All will be well."

After she had spoken her message, I felt her withdraw. For long moments Helena and I looked across the table at one another stunned. We both knew something incredible had happened. When Gail could finally open her eyes, she was crying with relief. "I felt her... I felt her wings on my face!" she said in disbelief. "I heard her speak inside my head."

"That was me," I answered uncertainly. "She used my voice."

"No, no, it wasn't you. When you first started speaking I heard you. Then I stopped hearing anything with my outside ears. I swear it. I heard her voice inside my head! She spoke to me!" Helena and I looked at Gail in amazement. What had really happened?

In the days and weeks to come, a miracle occurred. Gail began to heal in a totally unexpected way. Within six weeks the bandages came off. Two months later she had healed from all of her second and third degree burns with only the faintest scar left on the inside of one of her arms, almost like a gentle reminder of the Angels who had overseen her accident. The doctors told her it was a miracle, plain and simple. "What have you done?" they insisted. "You have no scars! We don't understand it!"

"It wasn't me that did it," she answered softly. "It was the voice of my Angels."

The Angel of Death

At a friend's wedding that same Fall, I received news that an actor friend of mine had become seriously ill with AIDS. His name was Stanton, and he was a fun, handsome, irrepressible man of about 32. We had been friends for more than a decade. During the wedding, friends who had kept up with him in more recent years came over to tell me that he was in the hospital in Texas and had been given 24 hours to live. I was shocked. I didn't even know he was sick.

I suggested a healing circle in absentee, and five or six of us gathered on the patio outside of the main festivities to send him prayers. We called in the White Light and placed Stanton in the middle of the circle. We called upon his Higher Self to be present and to receive the energy we would send, and one by one we went around the circle and spoke to him as if he were there. We told him how much we loved him. We told him how much his sweet nature had enriched our lives. We sent him healing energy with our hands, and then we closed with a prayer. No one expected that he would live out the week.

Six weeks later I got a phone call. Stanton was still alive. He had been moved to a hospital in Atlanta and could see visitors. I hung up the phone in amazement, wondering what horrors I could expect when I went to see him. That afternoon I left work and went to see him.

The room was dark and hushed. All the blinds had been pulled. He lay asleep on the bed, and as I entered the room I could hear the sound of his soft, labored breathing. I stood there for a full minute before I realized someone else was with me. A woman shifted in the chair beside the bed. I hadn't seen her before.

"How is he?" I asked softly.

"He's blind, you know. He's also not very lucid and he doesn't recognize people too often."

I nodded, uncertain what to say.

"I'm going to go," she stood up stretching. "Don't expect him to recognize you." She closed the door on her way out.

What good could I do here? I wondered. AIDS was a ravaging disease and Stanton's immune system had obviously gone way beyond anything the doctors could do. I opened my arms to the heavens and closed my eyes. I began to pray. I saw him in my mind's eye as I last remembered him, whole and strong, laughing and warm. That was the Stanton I knew. I could only ask to be made a vehicle for God's love. I had little hope that he would survive.

As I began to pray I felt as if a soft white-gold light descended into the room. Without thought, my hands began to work over his body, making motions that meant nothing to my conscious mind, but seemed to be directed from an entirely different source. After about ten minutes Stanton suddenly spoke up. "Who's there?" he whispered. I didn't even know he was awake.

"It's me, Stanton — Tricia."

He smiled slightly into the darkened room, but did not try to see me. I knew then that he really was blind, but he was conscious and lucid. "How are you, Tricia?" he asked me.

Tears sprang to my eyes. "Better than you, at the moment, my friend." I leaned and kissed him on the forehead.

"What were you doing a minute ago?" he asked me. How had he known I was "doing" anything? He had been asleep. I had been silent. His Spirit must have called him back into the body because of the energy work I was doing.

"I was doing some healing work on you," I answered. "I hope you don't mind." He tried to laugh, but it came out as a gurgle. "I think I need all of that I can get right now."

"Do you want me to continue?"

"Please."

I continued to work over him for another twenty minutes. During that time the white-gold light increased and I began to faintly see the figure of a Being at the foot of the bed. He was translucent and seemed to emit a soft, pulsing light. The figure had dark blonde, curly hair and a face of great serenity. His countenance was filled with patience. I said nothing to Stanton, however, not wanting to alarm him. When I was done and he was asleep again, I crept out of the room.

I called Helena the next day. "You have to go with me to the hospital," I said to her. "There's a friend of mine who needs your help." She agreed to meet me there the next afternoon. I said nothing about the Angel, waiting to see what Helena would experience. Together we worked over him for about thirty minutes. When we were done, we kissed him good-bye and left the room.

"Did you see all that white-gold light in the room?" Helena exclaimed as soon as we left.

I smiled. "Yes, and the last time I was here, I even saw an Angel, but I didn't see one this time. Do you suppose it is his Angel of Death?"

"They are waiting for him to pass on," she said wisely. "But he doesn't want to let go, does he?"

Sudden emotion filled my throat, and I could not answer. I thought about that all week long. Why wouldn't Stanton let go? His body had degenerated to such a point that even if he lived, his life would be torture. I didn't understand why he was clinging so fiercely to life. I decided that I would ask him the next time I went. But it was three weeks before I could get back to the hospital. I must confess that going there was hard for me. I felt so inadequate. I felt helpless to mend the pain or heal the sick. What good did I really do?

The City of Lights

It was just before Christmas when I made my last visit. Stanton's parents were in the hall and I spoke with them for awhile, telling them how much his life had meant to so many. I also told them that I wanted to try a healing for him, but I didn't know if it would work. They wept behind their hands and nodded. I went into the room alone.

"Stanton," I said, after we had greeted one another. "I don't exactly know how to ask this, but ... why are you still hanging on? Why don't you just go ahead and cross over?"

He struggled for a moment and then said quite clearly. "I'm afraid. I don't know what will happen to me if I go."

I held his hand and nodded. Now I understood. So many of us don't remember the nightly voyages we take to the other side, so death seems like a chasm we cannot fathom crossing. But because I had learned to bring back conscious memory of those nightly trips, I did not fear death — I welcomed it. I knew it was only a window through which our spirits floated, and that once beyond the heavy pulls of the body, we soared effortlessly into realms more glorious than human words can say. It all made sense now. "Would you like to go and see what is waiting for you on the other side?" I asked him gently.

His jaw fell open. A long moment in which his heartbeat could be measured. "How would I do that?"

"It isn't very hard. You're out there a lot of the time these days anyway, floating in and out of contact with the higher worlds. Simply close your eyes and follow the sound of my voice. Follow the sound of my voice."

His eyelids closed and he began to breathe. "At the foot of your bed stands an Angel, Stanton. He has blonde hair and he is one who has known you for a long, long time. We are going to ask this Angel to come and lift you from your body, and together the three of us are going to travel into the Inner Worlds where you will be living when you leave this Earth."

I looked to the foot of the bed and did not see the Angel, but that soft gold light was coming in from above. Suddenly the Angel was hovering above Stanton's bed, outstretched as if he was flying. I saw him reach down a hand. "Take his hand now, Stanton. He is reaching out to meet you. It is safe to reach back. Take his hand. He is offering you a preview of what will be in the days ahead."

Stanton's spirit rose up out of his physical form. I could see it as an astral glow. He hesitated for just a moment and then saw the Angel just above the bed. He placed his hand in the hand of his Guardian. The Angel smiled. Stanton was too amazed to smile back. I closed my eyes, hoping that I would be able to follow them, that I would be allowed to go on the journey to the other side too.

As if watching a movie scene, they lifted up through the ceiling. Then we were all suddenly in a cloud-filled vista moving through layers of white-gold light. In the distance I saw the buildings of what appeared to be a city. "That is where we are going," I whispered to Stanton. "It is the City of Lights."

Without warning, we were suddenly over the huge foyer of a large open hall. Tall pillars went up several stories in the air. The floor was made of marble. There were children everywhere. They were laughing and pushing eagerly at the teacher for attention. The teacher was a pretty, dark-haired woman, and she was teaching some sort of art to them. This is a school, I realized, a school for creative arts!

The Angel turned to look at Stanton. He spoke no words, but the message was clear. "We are waiting for you." I looked down into the room again, and I saw Stanton in the future. He would be teaching the children all sorts of creative arts. His theatrical background, and all the things he had learned in this life would be put to good use here in this temple. I knew the other teachers had been waiting for him to take his place there for several months. Only his own stubborn will and fear had prevented him from taking that step.

"They have a job for you, Stanton," I whispered in his ear. "And it's something you're going to love."

Stanton took a long look, and I could feel his fear turning to understanding. "There is no death." I heard his thought. "This is not the end."

After awhile the Angel returned us to the room. When Stanton came back into his body, he began to weep. "I had no idea it would be so beautiful! I had no idea they would actually want me ... want me to teach children in heaven."

I laughed and squeezed his hand. "Looks like they were willing to wait for you, too," I said in wonder. "There's nothing to be afraid of anymore."

Two days later Stanton passed over, taking the wholeness of his spirit with him and leaving the shell of his worn out body behind.

Karmic Promises

 question of where people go when they die is an immense one. It's something that every mortal person thinks about at one time or another, because naturally, being mortal, we will someday cross to the other side. Over the years, I have had many insights into this profound mystery. Today in our society the "near-death" experience is finally being given serious examination. Courageous people like Dannion Brinkley and Melvin Morse have shared their stories in best-selling books like "Saved By The Light" and "Closer To The Light".

Out of body travel to the Inner Planes allows us to visit those other worlds as well, and every night when we sleep, each of us travels to those astral landscapes and beyond. At the lowest levels of the Astral plane, we experience nightmares. At the next levels, we "project" a subjective reality based on our hopes, fears and wishes, this in turn creates the appearance of a world, which is a reflection of our subconscious voice. Many people never remember dreaming past this level of insubstantial reality, yet in truth we often do.

If we ascend to the higher vibrational levels of the Astral plane and above, we enter worlds that have an externally manifested reality, just as our Earth does now. In other words, we can actually visit places that exist — planets, temples, gardens and schools where those who have passed over during death reside.

After Death

Where do we each go when we die? It's a good question.

Each of us is an individual, thus we are each led by our Guides to that place which is most appropriate for our greatest growth. Yes, we do join with loved ones on the other side, although we may not stay with them long because our own needs for growth are different from theirs. Yes, beloved pets will sometimes wait for us before continuing their own reincarnational cycles, moving from group souls into individual consciousness. And yes, we are greeted by such Beings of Light that their vast compassion is beyond anything we know of as normal human love. It is unconditional and non-judgmental, and it is completely honest in its review of where we are in our unfoldment as spiritual beings.

Many wonder if there is anything to do on the other side. Absolutely! That's like asking if there's anything to do over here. No, you don't have to earn a living or do a job. But souls often choose to work or play at something they love. I have read for souls who are studying at Universities on the other side. In one reading, a woman's recently deceased husband was learning five Earth languages in such a setting. This was in preparation for the work he will do in his next incarnation here on Earth. He plans to be an international mediator in the government arena. His wife smiled broadly when I told her this. She said that he had worked for the government over a decade in the area of public relations and always wanted to learn foreign languages.

Once I read for a widow whose husband had been a doctor. He had followed traditional medicine, resisting her suggestions to look into alternative healing techniques. I did not know any of this. I saw that on the other side he is now studying the effects of light and sound healing on the human body. His wife was thrilled. This was the very thing she had tried to get him to look into for years before he died!

On one occasion I read for a woman whose sister had dropped

dead of a heart attack two weeks earlier. Both sisters where in their early thirties, so the death had been a shock to everyone. The first thing I saw when I held the deceased woman's picture was a beautiful monastery, similar to those of the Franciscan order. There a "monk" came forward and addressed me, saying that the young woman was spending a lot of time in their gardens still making her initial adjustments. The living sister gasped. "For the last six months," she said excitedly, "my sister kept having these dreams of a Franciscan monastery. She said she loved the gardens. She must have known that she was going there soon."

Occasionally I will see a deceased loved one visiting those who have stayed behind. This is usually only allowed for a brief period. Then they must get on about the business of their own lives in the heavenly worlds. I did not know when I began doing these readings that tracking a soul after death was even possible. My first inkling happened in the middle of someone dying.

The Nudge of Spirit

I had been taking photographs of a client one afternoon, and my Angels gave me a nudge to offer to read for him. As a commercial photographer, I usually play down my clairvoyant abilities, because it gets awkward trying to explain exactly what I see to people who haven't come to see me for this reason. I've developed a "dimmer switch" on my abilities, and I turn them down whenever it's inappropriate. Imagine for example, doing a photo shoot for a corporate client like Coca-Cola or Turner communications and suddenly seeing a succession of life times flash before your eyes! It's hard to say, "Excuse me Mr. Vice President, but did you know that you were once a French knight in the Middle Ages, and that you killed some of the very people you're having trouble with in your office today?" Very distracting, if you see what I mean.

Yet when Spirit insists on nudging me hard, it is usually because the person's Guides have something urgent to say. So I will generally take the plunge and cautiously inquire. To my surprise, most people are very interested and have even had flashes of their own past lives. They often keep silent because they don't want the rest of the world to think they are crazy, never realizing that if only we all knew how many people are "in the spiritual closet" we would each be more willing to come out.

So finally, I gave into this prompting and said to my client, "You probably don't know this, John but I do readings for people. For some reason I'm being told to offer one to you."

He was thrilled. He had always wanted a reading. Could he invite his wife? "Of course," I reassured him. "Come to my house at 7:00 tonight."

Scanning the Records

They were a lovely couple, John and Laura, in their late 40's, stable and open to spiritual growth. Throughout the reading I got the nagging feeling that I wasn't really tapping into what their Angels wanted me to see, but I didn't know what to do about it. We covered their primary emotional issues, their past life karma as it related to this life, and the relationships with their two sons. Finally they got up to leave, thanking me profusely.

Over the last drops of tea in the kitchen, Laura confessed that this reading had meant a great deal to her because just the day before, she had gotten word that her brother had been diagnosed with cancer. A shiver ran through me. This was it! She went on. He had been given between two weeks and two months to live. I knew now that this was the real reason I had been sent to read for them!

"Do you have a picture of your brother?" I asked, for I can read the etheric imprint of an individual through just a photograph.

"No, I wish I did," she said regretfully.

"We may not be able to understand it from our mortal perspective," I told her, "but everyone at the Soul level, chooses when they will leave this Earth. Soul knows when it is the right time to die."

Laura began to cry in sweet, sad sobs. "Why would he... why would a man in the prime of his life ... decide to just ... check out like this?"

My shivers got stronger. "Give me your hand," I said. "I think I can access your brother's records without a picture because of your love for him. Let me see."

Crossing Over

I closed my eyes and brought in the Christ light. I surrounded myself, Laura, and her brother David in it. Images of a handsome, fair-haired man appeared. He was speaking with a slender dark-haired woman. Both were in their late forties. I saw a large house with one girl child. As I described this, Laura told me I was seeing her brother, his wife, and their only daughter. He was saying good-bye. He was going through the list of all the things she would need to be aware of at his death: the will, the mortgage, their child's future. Then as I watched, something happened. I could actually see him lift up out of his body, just as Stanton had, except this time no silver cord kept him tied. He passed through the ceiling of the room. As he went into the sky, three luminous beings came to meet him and over all of them was the cloak of a white Angelic presence.

The three beings were loved ones he had known from the past, and they seemed to be coming in from the heavens themselves. One was an elderly gentleman, a mentor he had known as a friend from another life time. They immediately greeted one another in pleasure. The second was his grandmother who had passed over during his life on Earth. She had come as part of the welcoming party.

And the third spirit was a radiant young woman who greeted him in great joy and tenderness. From the moment he saw her, he never looked back. She was the soul mate he had never found in this life. Their shared joy was radiance itself. They embraced. He was in ecstasy. As they came together, I saw the enormity of their karmic promise so long ago made. Before he had incarnated into this life, these two souls had made an agreement that when the time came for her to reincarnate on Earth once again, he would return with her. That way they could grow up, find each other and be married. He was dying now because she was coming back into a physical body! By staying on Earth, he would have been too old to be her mate.

Laura's eyes filled with joy. She had always known the unrequited longing in her brother's heart. All his life he had sought this soul mate and never found her. "I'm so glad!" she cried aloud. "He'll be truly happy at last!" Some five hours later John and Laura called me at home. Their voices were awed.

"When we got home," they told me over the telephone, "Sara, David's wife had called us. There was a message on our answering machine."

"Yes," I urged them. "Go on."

"David died," Laura told me with awe in her voice. There was no fear as she said it, and only a trace of sadness. "Sara left the time on the recorder. Tricia, he died at the exact moment that you were doing the reading for him."

I realized I was holding my breath. What a miracle! I had been allowed to see the moment of his passing into the arms of his Angel and his reunion with the soul mate he had dreamed of for so long!

Angels in England

Winter following the year I first met the Angels in New York City, a wonderful thing happened. I went to England for the first time. Now England, as you may know, is the place of many ancient holy sites. Well-known legends of Stonehenge, Glastonbury, and Camelot abound there. For thousands of years the Celts and Druids kept alive the ancient knowledge of the magnetic ley lines that run across the planet Earth, and they designed the holy sites of the ancient world around them. Authors like John Michell have chronicled such things in his book "View From Atlantis", and David Wood's extraordinary book "Genisis" lays out a complex system of such sacred geometry all over Europe.

I did not know much about this at the time that I first visited England, but I experienced it directly while I was there. The more recent faith of Christianity was very aware of these magnetic grid points at the time that they built the great cathedrals. They placed the churches carefully on many of these timeless spots. I knew going over there that I wanted to visit three of these power places specifically: Stonehenge, Saint Paul's Cathedral in London, and Canterbury Cathedral in the small village of Canterbury. As it turned out I got a glimpse into far more than I ever imagined.

As you may recall, I had been looking at the time track for years, but I could not always access information at will. England and the initiation that it produced changed something fundamental inside of me. Afterward, because of what transpired, I found that I was able to tap into such visions of the past and future at will.

Time Shift

We rode a train to Stonehenge. I was with the parents of my fiancé at the time, and they had agreed to take me on a day trip to this sacred site. The fence that was later erected around Stonehenge had not been put up yet. We walked the perimeter slowly, soaking in the feel of the ancient stones, and then to give me some privacy, his parents left me alone.

I sat with my back against one of the huge stone monoliths at the entry way, closing my eyes. I could feel the power of the ancient block itself, seeping through the shirt on my back. The power of these stones was enormous. Even the mass was ponderous. I wondered how long they had been there and who had brought them into such perfect astronomical alignment thousands of years before. I pulled my hands out of my lap and touched the rock behind me with my fingertips. It was cold and hard and rough. I stretched my senses into it, wondering what images might come to me.

Suddenly everything grew very quiet. A moment before, I was sure there had been murmured voices from the small clumps of walking tourists. The faint smell of smoke came to my nostrils. I opened my eyes. Everyone was gone! In the distance I saw something burning. Pillars of black plumed smoke curled up into the sky, and I could just make out the faint cries of people shouting.

I got to my knees, back still pressed against the stone. A strange energy came over the circle. I looked back at the station across the road where my friends had gone. The station had totally vanished! In fact the road itself had changed. It was no longer a highway. It was just dirt. Far in the distance near the smoke, I could see tiny people running. They were shouting. What was happening? Suddenly the realization hit me. Time had shifted. I was in another century!

I looked around the stones, trying to sense the differences. Had all of these stones been standing before? I couldn't remember. Then my eyes alighted on a figure standing in front of one of the monoliths. I gasped. He was huge and translucent, but distinct from the monolith itself. As I looked, the realization dawned on me that he had wings. Without warning, he lifted his finger to his lips, as if trying to tell me something. The gleam in his eyes was piercing. My mouth dropped open. I was looking at an Angel!! His curly brown hair fell to his shoulders. His wings were slightly spread. A smile played upon his lips. He looked directly at me, finger to his lips. The gesture seemed so peculiar that I didn't know what it meant. Then as I watched, he ran his finger down the cleft at the center of his top lip and lowered his hand.

What did it mean? I got to my feet slowly, almost hypnotized with awe. My back was still pressed against the stone. Finally as I managed to move forward, I broke contact with the stone. Immediately, everything shifted. I was back in the 20th century. The Angel was gone!

Tourists who had not been there a moment before drifted lazily around the circle. The murmur of their soft voices reached my ears. I stood in the center for a long moment, dazed, trying to decide exactly what had happened. My eyes returned again and again to the place where the Angel had been. Was he still there? I couldn't see him now. I didn't know. I walked back to the monolith I had sat against. I touched it, then looked around the circle.

Nothing changed. I slowly walked over to the Angel's monolith. "Are you still there?" I said aloud to him, but there was no answer.

After several minutes my friends found me, looking perplexed and confused. The Angel had put his finger to his lips. Then he had lowered his hand with a smile. Was there a secret to be kept? Should I keep the experience to myself? I was not sure, so I never spoke a word of it to my friends. It was only later that I realized what it could mean, and it is because of that, and what happened after, that I share it now.

The Memories Awaken

I went to Canterbury the next week. We stayed in the small house of a couple of my fiancé's friends. It had been a barn in olden times, now converted into a cottage. We slept on the floor of their living room on a pull-out bed. A ley line passed directly through the room, and I had wild dreams all night.

The couple had three girls of varying ages, and the youngest was an eight -year-old. She danced for us one night in the living room, moving wildly around the large braided throw-rug in the fashion of little girls everywhere. As I watched her, I began to see powerful overlays of lives in earlier centuries. She had been a ballerina in Paris a century before when she had been in love with a violinist. She had been a belly dancer hundreds of years earlier in a harem. I told my fiancé what I saw, but of these visions I said nothing to the parents.

Later the little girl told us that she had something special to show us. She ran upstairs and came back with a violin. "I'm going to learn to play," she said sweetly. "Then I'll be adored by everyone." I knew that this wish had begun during her lifetime in Paris and in this life she would once again meet her great love from that century. Over supper, the parents told us that she and her older sisters used to dress up in Turkish outfits when they were much younger, pretending to be belly dancers in a sultan's harem. They even had exotic names for each other in those identities.

I shook my head and laughed, looking at my fiancé. He smiled knowingly. We had no doubt that these girls had all incarnated together in some distant lifetime as belly-dancers. Here they were in England, weaving the threads of their lives together again. The next morning we said good-bye to our friends, marveling at the synchronicities of life. We returned to London the next day.

Ancient Questions

I was alone in England for a couple of weeks before I had to return to the States. Mark was working. I wandered the city by myself, exploring it like a child. The city itself brought up great emotion in me, and as romantic as it was, it stirred life times of complex feelings. I had no doubt that I had lived here before, even if I couldn't recall the details. I wanted to visit St. Paul's Cathedral before I left London, yet it took awhile to find it on my own. Once I did, I knew why I had come.

It was spectacular. Large white, marble statues of life-sized Angels filled the Church. Their features were so perfectly carved that one would swear that in a moment the Angels would come to life. The gaze of their countenances held me spell-bound. I walked around the huge-winged Beings. I thought about the Angel I had seen at Stonehenge. I traced the curve of their cheeks, the outlines of their graceful arms, even the seeming transparency of the fabric they wore.

I had no words for this. Certainly these long-gone artists of another era had had their own Divine visions of Angelic hosts. Otherwise, how else could they have carved them with such perfection?

Who were the Angels really? I wondered. Were they tall or human-sized? Did they have wings like the one on the angel at Stonehenge, or did the glow of their auric fields simply look like wings extending on either side of their bodies? I did not remember seeing wings on either of the healing Angels, yet there had been a strong glow of light around both their bodies. Were they male or female, or androgynous, beyond the desire to love one another with their sexuality? They seemed to have specific gender orientations, but did this mean that they could love each other as humans do? And was there something wrong if they did?

I walked around these columnar figures, so vast, so majestic. Had these Angelic Beings once been human like us? Had they achieved such Divine consciousness that they no longer needed to incarnate in human form? Instead, had they volunteered to help out their younger cousins on Earth? I did not know the answers to these questions, but I wanted to.

I sat and meditated by the statue of an Angel speaking with a human. Such love the Angel had in its eyes. Did everyone have a guardian Angel? Were certain Angels sent for special purposes? If this was true, how could there be so many spirits and how could we be so oblivious to them all around us? I wanted these Angels to tell me.

Suddenly I remembered a story I had read long ago of the Cavern Angel. This is the Angel, so the legend goes, that places his finger on your lips just before you descend to Earth. When he does so, he marks your upper lip with his finger. Then you forget who you are. You forget the soul agreements you have made to fulfill your life's purpose. You forget the loved ones you have known in the heavenly kingdoms. And perhaps most importantly, you forget all that has happened to you before this moment.,

I thought of my vision at Stonehenge. The Angel had put a finger to his lips. Then he had removed it and smiled at me. What could he have meant? Was this a foreshadowing to the human race? Are we soon to remember who we are? Was this his way of lifting the veils of memory, breaking the seals of silence? Are we soon to remember who we really are and why we have come to Earth?

It was only later, after I had returned from England, that I realized I could now access the records of anyone I met. At last the Akashic had been opened to me in the deepest of ways, and the door to what was to come had been unsealed.

But there in the Cathedral, I did not know this and so I knelt in awe at the feet of the two Angels. Their faces looked down at me with such patience, such unconditional love.

"Answer my prayers," I pleaded with them silently. "Just please answer my prayers."

Decent Into the World

Rough Waters and
Ancient Answers

When I returned from England, my life took a drastic turn. I went through several difficult years of being divested of things I had taken for granted in my life. My engagement to the man in England was called off in a most painful way. Since we were 6,000 miles apart it was difficult, at best, to attempt a reconciliation. So after several frustrating months we gave the relationship up.

I had built a large, expensive photographic studio in Atlanta that had been my income base for several years. When I decided to marry Mark, I had given notice on that space. Returning to Atlanta, I no longer had a studio in which to operate. At home, my bright, three-story house had been a source of joy and pride to me for several years. Now because of the studio instability, I found it difficult to meet the $2,100 a month mortgage payment. I finally sold my house at a $15,000 loss, which I agreed to pay back for the next seven years of my life.

All of this forced me to take serious stock of my life. What was really happening behind these events? What did I think was most important? Money, love, stability, achievement? Had I become so enmeshed in my advertising career, my material belongings, and my symbols of status that I had somehow gotten my priorities mixed up? I realized at one point that I had gone from owning my big, beautiful expensive things to having my things own me. I was no longer working for joy. I was working to survive. Life seemed like a huge struggle, and I wondered how it had all turned out this way.

I tried to meditate, but often failed to find any stillness at all. When I could sit by my altar, I would hear the words, "Let go, let go." Was I to let go of my house, my career and my relationships all at once? These were the ways I had come to know my identity. These were the symbols of success I had worked for so long and hard. Wasn't this what my upbringing had taught me? Have a good job, a good house, a good mate and you'll live happily ever after. If I gave up these things, what would happen to me? Who would I be, if I was not all these expressions of respectability.

Ancient Wisdom

Years later, I heard a story which spoke directly to this dilemma. It was told to me by a friend who had studied with a Native American holy man who was more than a hundred years old. "Why is it," my friend had asked, "that the society of our people is so troubled by violence, struggle and insecurity?"

"It is because you teach your children false values," the old Shaman had answered. "You teach your young to strive for money, power and sex. These values will always make a person feel dissatisfied. Who feels they can have enough money, when money can be taken from them so easily? Who feels they can have enough power, if power in their society is linked to money and the acquisition of material goods which may be washed away in a moment's notice? And sex - your society parades the ideal of sex as an unattainable allure, so that deep down many feel they will never be satisfied with one partner. There is always a more beautiful one on the television set. With these false values, you are always striving to attain that which you cannot keep. And it does not make you ever feel safe or worthy as human beings."

My friend was silent for a long time. "What values should we strive for?" he finally asked.

"All over the world, native peoples were once taught the value of service, humility and devotion as their highest ideals. This promotes a sense of self-worthiness. One can always be of service to another and feel good about one's self. One can always be more devoted to his mate, his tribe, his ideals or to the Great Creator. And lastly, the value of humility allows us to remember our place in the circle of life. We are all important. We all have something to contribute. These values bring each of us the one thing your society is so hungry for — happiness and peace of mind."

Letting Go of Ourselves

At the time my life was falling apart around my ears. I had not heard this story, so things were not so clear to me then. I was being pulled by the voice of my wise inner self who knew this wisdom. It said, "Do not struggle so. You will be all right." But I was also being pulled by the voice of years of social training which I had accepted as real. This exercised a powerful grip on my psyche. I did not want to let my parents down. I did not want to let myself down. To have reached a success plateau on the ladder of achievement and find that I might have to descend a few rungs, or even go in a different direction entirely, was unsettling and hard.

As I sat by my altar I prayed in desperation. "Let go," the voice answered, but I was not sure what it meant. Was there something deeper being asked of me? Let go of what? Of everything? Were these trophies being melted away so that I might realize another identity within myself?

I came to feel that this intense physical and emotional stripping away of my world was symbolic of something greater. Maybe I was being asked to "let go" of some belief system that everyone else (including me) had accepted but that really had no spiritual worth.

Maybe I was being asked to relinquish some kind of control I imagined I had over my life. Perhaps the key was complete surrender to another way of being

Revelation

In the meantime, in spite of the emotional pain, or perhaps because of it, my attention was turning to spiritual matters. I felt the foundations of my life shifting, and I knew that in some profound way I was dying only to be reborn. Death is a painful process if we resist it, and as stubborn as we humans are, we usually do resist. But letting go means allowing the flow of our lives to take us into the new moment - the undefined, unknown moment, where all that we have known about ourselves transforms, and we become more than what we ever dreamed.

At the time I did not know this, but I was compelled by the difficulty of my circumstance to rely more and more on inner trust. This meant listening to the subtle nudges of my intuition. It meant trusting that there was some innate wisdom operating behind the scenes, even if I couldn't see it.

I was directed from this time on to do spiritual readings for others, at first uncertainly, and then with more and more confidence. The way it worked was this: I would meet someone, often for the first time, someone I knew nothing about. We might be at a social function, or they could be coming into my life for photographs. As I looked at them I would begin to get visual overlays. Often they were of past lifetimes. I would see their faces change, become aware of them in different centuries, even hear dialogue, music or background sounds. I was literally being shown a movie overlay of who they were, where they had been, and what road they had come down. Sometimes I would see deceased loved ones around them or the presence of an Angelic being.

Without conscious intent, I would automatically begin to receive information, and Spirit would nudge me to share this. I would clear my throat a few times and say something like, "I don't know if you believe in this sort of thing, but I sometimes see past lives, and for some reason your Guides are showing me things about you that you might want to know. Do you want to hear this?"

Invariably they did. Since we had only just met, the results would be as astonishing to me as they were to them. These visions would create a tremendous "ah-ha!" of realization. Afterward, they would tell me just how much sense they made from the perspective of what was now going on in their lives. We would marvel at the synchronicity of the thing, and the day would go on.

Karmic Bread Crumbs

Now the readings were often around the confusion of personal relationships which are usually karmic. This means that these were people from the past with whom my client had interacted. I would also be shown emotional and mental patterns that were at play in their lives which they had not outgrown. These patterns would literally be "out-pictured" in front of me, as I saw the past lives which had originally set them in motion.

This new way of seeing opened up an enormous level of understanding. I realized for the first time the incredible beauty of the mechanisms of karma in our lives. As I followed someone from lifetime to lifetime I knew I was following the trail of emotional and physical bread crumbs down the path towards their enlightenment. Issues which had once been obscured and dark became light when seen from a greater perspective. Traumas became healed. Things that made no sense from our limited human perspective in the Now took on the stature of revelation as I watched the Divine Wisdom of the Universe operating behind the scenes.

The true meaning of Karma became very clear to me. Karma is simply the inertia of our thoughts manifesting in our lives. It is the momentum of past deeds - kindness or cruelties - allowing us to balance our misconceptions to come to a higher state of Grace and Love.

In the process of these revelations, I began to see a most peculiar and wonderful thing — the presence of Spirit Guides around the person I was reading for. These Divine support systems took many forms, not only those that I expected. And so in the next chapter, we will take a look at the beauty and diversity of those who love us, those who have walked with us down all of the many centuries of our unfoldment.

Spirit Guides Surround Us

 of the most profound things I discovered was that all of us do have spiritual Guides, whether we are in touch with them or not. They come in many forms besides that which we have come to call Angelic. Each of these "mentor" energies is part of the Divine plan of conscious Beings helping those less aware move into the Light. Individually, each of these spiritual forces may be recognized through tuning into the etheric fields of the person I am reading. They actually "sit" (or stand) in their auric fields. Often unknown to the person's conscious mind, these spiritual mentors regularly hold discourse with the individual at an energetic level, nudging, suggesting and encouraging him or her toward a higher spiritual purpose.

The Ancestral Spirit

The Ancestral Spirit may come as no surprise to those from the East, but it was something I had never considered until I encountered it in a reading. Ancestral spirits are the spirits of human beings who have lived and died on Earth and now remain for some benign purpose to help the living. Many of our forefathers believed that powerful spiritual masters, saints and holy men continue to protect temples after passing beyond the veils of death. This is true.

Some believe that these ancestral "great ones" reincarnate into a particular tribe again and again to guide the people, just as Tibetans believe that the Dalai Lama returns many times to serve their faith. The Eastern world has temples to honor these Ancestors, and many families even have private altars in their homes to honor those who have passed on. The Ancestors, they believe, can bless you or curse you, so it is important to send them prayers and remember to honor them.

While I see that most people who die continue their journeys in the other dimensions and have little to do with this world after death, certainly sending loving prayers to them is healing. And on occasion these Ancestral Spirits return to interact with us in times of crisis. In the Americas, indigenous tribal peoples, including the Mayans and Native Americans, rarely speak the names of the dead, believing that to use their names is to summon them from the other worlds. Mayans call them the abuwelos and abuwelas, the grandfathers and grandmothers, and hold them in great respect. Many tribes, in fact, believe that their greatest leaders still live on in the land protecting it from those who would do it harm. I have experienced these grandfather/grandmother spirits first-hand a number of times.

In this country, we hardly think of Ancestral Spirits at all, or if we do, we call them ghosts. This is because we have been taught that we live only one life and afterward go to Heaven or Hell for all of eternity. The idea of a spirit living on without a body is usually reserved for discussions of spooks, poltergeists, and scary stories around the camp fires. But the traumatized souls who make up the astral world of ghosts are but a small percentage of the whole, and most who dwell in spirit realms close to Earth are far more positively oriented.

Ancestral spirits who have chosen to stay on Earth are those who have a particular mission. After death, instead of going on into the other realms of Light, they stay to oversee a particular person or location as a job assignment. Often this has to do with helping someone they love get through a difficult part of his or her life. It may have to do with personal healing, grief work, the growth of an artistic endeavor, the raising of a special child, or even the gaining of a particular type of knowledge. Once that task is completed, they return to the Light of their own evolutionary growth pattern.

Ancestral spirits are usually those we have known in this lifetime - a grandmother, a mother, a child, a grandfather, a mentor or a husband. Sometimes they may even be a relative we have never met, but who has a strong karmic bond with us. Many times, our very genetic code itself is connected to them and they are present to pass on specific talents or information.

Ancestral Spirits can effect us in a variety of ways. They may act as invisible confidants, companions or the gentle nudge of a conscience when we most need it. They still retain much of the emotional qualities we knew when they were living, so they do have distinct personalities. Yet most have evolved to a greater understanding of the Universe, since they now "know" there is life on the other side.

If you find you have Ancestral Spirits around you, it is appropriate to communicate with them and find out why they are here. Their presence may be temporary or meant to last a lifetime. If they are merely visiting, it is best to communicate about their mission, and then to ultimately let them go on about the business of their own evolution in the higher worlds. The love they bear us is wonderful, but our desire for them to stay with us can hold them back from focusing on their own personal growth. In the end, we must bless and release them to their own spiritual lives.

Muses

I was quite amazed to find that the legends of Muses have a basis in fact. These thoroughly delightful, loving guides are really Angels of creativity who act as guides for artists, musicians and the like. Muses do not choose to serve everyone, although one can attract a Muse by the joyful open hearted desire to create. They are diverse and playful, usually found around artists devoted to cultivating their many inspired gifts. They may remain with a soul through multiple lifetimes, returning again and again to enhance one's artistic work.

The Muses I have met have all been female. Perhaps there are other kinds, but I have not met them. They travel in groups of two or more, arriving in sociable clusters of three or four. When a person is blessed with such a benevolent Spirit, you can bet there are others nearby.

Muses are versed in every aspect of creativity. One may be adept at transmitting musical compositions. Human recipients may find themselves hearing music in their heads, humming a lot or having a tendency to be involved with some aspect of musical work. Another Muse may deal with the cadences of poetry and rhythm. A third may influence talent in dance or movement. A fourth will bring color or painting. A fifth works with sculpture. A sixth with touch or healing. These very social beings love to communicate. They exist in great creative joy at the higher dimensional levels and descend into a person's auric field only to act as catalysts for artistic inspiration. Playful and loving, they delight in all manner of positive creativity and if you are one of those blessed enough to have a Muse (or two) as a spiritual companion, do not neglect her. She can bring her sisters to bear on any creative endeavor of your heart.

Animal Spirits

Indigenous people all over the world have displayed great knowledge in interacting with a type of spiritual guide rarely mentioned by those with strong scientific paradigms. In fact, so far has our culture come from our connection with the animal kingdom who lives with us that many do not even comprehend the idea of Power Animals.

Yet most of us can easily name one or two animals with whom we share great admiration and affection. Examined more closely, these may be subtle clues to our own Animal Spirit totems.

Native Americans who were deeply aligned with the pulse of the Great Spirit through the harmonics of nature looked upon all animals as sacred. They considered them friends, allies and beings of intelligence. Animals were not just pets to share our lodges or meat to be eaten, but every animal was seen as part of a particular group spirit.

The spirit of Wolf, for example, is that of a teacher energy. Bear represents compassion and strength. Eagle stands for majesty and leadership. Hawk is messenger. Ant is industry. Coyote is humor and trickster. Deer is innocence and fear/trust. Antelope and buffalo represent self-sacrifice for the good of the whole. In this way Native Americans saw each life, no matter what its form, as sacred. Each being, whether human, four-footed or winged, contributes equally to the whole - something we in the western world could stand to remember.

Taken beyond the physical realms, the spirits of these animals represent a quality that is a teacher energy to the whole circle of life. In Native American stories of the earlier ages of humankind, it has been said that the animals were known to speak. But our ability to hear them telepathically was taken from us because we could not stand to hear them beg for mercy when we killed them. It has also been said that the powers and insights of animals can become guides for human beings, and that their appearance in our dreams and our waking lives is not insignificant. If we pay attention to them, they will offer nurturance, teaching and protection.

During the course of thousands of readings, I have seen that many, many human beings have animal Spirit power. They have the assistance and guidance of a particular soul group that is their friend and ally. By consciously acknowledging and working with that "over-soul" energy, we not only come into greater alignment with nature and the animal kingdom, but we come to claim those qualities in ourselves.

This was known in some European cultures as well. Athena, for example, had the owl as a totem energy. That ally gave her the power to see the truth, even in total darkness, just as an owl does. It was the sign of the clairvoyant. Apollo's radiant energy was represented by the majestic lion, still seen as the symbol of kingship throughout western Europe. The lion is aligned with truth. In ancient cultures lions sat beside the thrones of kings and queens and helped to detect the fear pheromones produced by those who came into the court for justice yet did not walk in truth. In Christianity, the Dove has long been the sign of the Christ consciousness, whether expressed through Mary or Jesus. The dove is the bringer of world peace. And in the early days of Christianity, the fish, which represented the incoming Piscean Age, was used as a symbol by the budding new religion. "May we be fishers of men," was a saying often heard in early Christian circles.

Animal energies are real. They exist in the Universe. Each of us can choose to be aware of them or not, but our perception (or lack of it) does not mean they do not exist. If there is one thing I have learned along the way, it is this simple truth.

God and Goddess Archetypes

The Archetypal realms are a very real aspect of Creation as well and have far greater influence on our lives than we may suspect. In fact, many of the oversoul energies that each of us is connected to are ancient expressions of Universal archetypes. Traditional psychology has cast this into the category of myth, but I have found through the direct appearance of these beings that these archetypes actually have life on the higher levels of reality. Thinkers like Carl Jung and Joseph Campbell were involved in extensive examinations of these ancient mythologies, trying to decipher the hidden meaning behind them. They wanted to know what our ancestors could have meant when they worshipped such Beings. Were these real, or were they projections of our collective unconscious? My experience would indicate that they are both.

While much of the Eastern world recognizes these archetypal beings, reconciling the existence of god and goddess archetypes with traditional Judeo/Christian teachings may initially challenge some of you. Yet, I have discovered that the creative force of the Universe manifests through the prism of countless expressions, including those we refer to as gods and goddesses. Just as the Angels act as a sort of spiritual task force to assist in the running of the Universe, so too do these primal archetypes of Creation act as part of a monadic pyramid overseeing specific evolutionary patterns for us all.

When I do a reading, sometimes I will see someone sits beneath the energies of one of these beautiful archetypes. What I mean by this is that his or her soul pattern is aligned with a specific expression of Divine Isness. It might be the Mary or Quan Yin matrix of the supreme Mother, the epitome of forgiveness and love. It might be the energies of Sophia or Athena, expressions of divine wisdom and fairness. As part of the monadic pyramid of oversoul energies, these beings could be said to oversee us, influencing and strengthening that which is already inherent in our very makeup.

Let me give you an example: a person whose very presence is bright, sunny, powerful and outgoing and who acts as a radiant healer for others might have emerged from the archetype of the Sun. This was once expressed on our world as the god Apollo. It was also expressed as Ra energy, Arthurian energy, and all solar gods who were "keepers of the land." Each of these solar expressions is unique, and for one who stands beneath the monad of this particular arche-typal being, he or she would be a radiant leader/healer of Earth. Similarly, a woman who is independent, nature-oriented, musical, sleek and athletic might stand beneath the archetype of the god-dess Diana, known as both healer, warrior and nature lover. Equally true, one who is concerned with law, fairness, government, struc-ture, teaching and large groups of people might stand beneath Athena's vibrational matrix.

Perceiving these soul correlations is not done with the logical mind. For me, it happens in an altered state of consciousness. When I do the reading, the archetype actually enters the room as a Being and speaks to me. Only then do I know how the qualities of that archetypal oversoul have influenced a person's destiny or endowed his or her with gifts.

Just who are these gods and goddesses? Are they real or merely the sub-text of our subconscious minds? Psychologists have many interpretations, seeking to understand how perfectly rational, ambitious, materialistic men and women like the Romans could have believed in such things. Some think these beings were the ancient world's way of explaining particular personality types, just as we now have psychological tests like the Myer-Briggs personality tests which tell us whether someone is introverted or extroverted, a feeler or a sensor, a thinker or intuitive. It is certainly one way to explain it.

Yet since I directly see, hear and feel these Beings who seem to have their own higher world existence *independent of us*, com-plete with names, provinces of influence, clothing, coloring, size, complex personalities, energetic alignments, and powers, I suspect it is more serious than subconscious projection. They are, in fact, every bit as complete as you or I but with a much larger sphere of influence and power. Because of this repeated evidence, I am com-pelled to consider that these Beings have their own existence in the higher worlds that we may be oblivious to in our day to day, rationally limited lives.

Is it not possible, I ask myself, that in the distant past these Beings were closer to Earth's vibrational field and thus could be perceived more easily? Perhaps Earth herself (and the people who lived on her) were closer to their dimensions, so the gap between us was smaller. Could some of them be considered ET's? Did they visit in space ships, or in inter-dimensional fields of transport that were far from modern technology? If we once could hear, see and interact with these higher vibrating beings in ancient times, could it not happen again? Their names are legend: Ishtar, Athena, Maat, Lilith, Apollo, Isis, Hera, Kali, Inanna, Ra, and Aphrodite. Perhaps in ages past, when this knowledge was better known, people actually saw and heard them. But once we densified and our scientific paradigms kicked in, it was no longer acceptable to even consider this kind of contact as a possibility. Thus, we closed the door to these octaves of understanding.

My belief is that they are opening again. Whatever they are, I know this: some individuals have very strong archetypal Guides working with them. And who is to say that by recognizing our connection with them, and honoring them as larger expressions of the Divine force, we do not all learn to embrace some larger portion of heaven?

Angels

Though we will speak of Angels in depth throughout the rest of this book, I cannot write a chapter on spirit guides without honoring them. They are truly the Shining Ones, each devoted to the upliftment of humankind. We each have Angelic guides. This I see when I read for people. Often a person may have two or even three. Personal Angels may seem more or less dormant in one's life, depending on one's level of self- awareness. The more awakened we be-come, the more we move into a conscious symbiotic relationship with Angels.

Our ability to sense angelic presences through sight, hearing, the feeling of a hand on our shoulder, or simply the abiding sense of knowing that everything is "all right," takes a little practice. Auto-matic writing, meditation and dialoguing can open the door to more direct communication with them and can literally change the way we operate in our day to day life.

Angels operate through economy. If it is less disruptive to get our attention by having a book fall off a shelf and land on our heads than by materializing in our bedrooms, that is the route they will take. They operate through subtlety. They will nudge someone to come to our aid when we are sick or need encouragement. They will nudge us if we are going in the wrong direction. And on occa-sion they will even call our names aloud.

There are countless stories of Angels taking human form and appearing to aid, nourish, comfort or provide for those in need. Some-times they are seen by those they are helping. Often only young people or those in altered states of stress see them. One story, for example, tells how such shining visitors accompanied the Pope when he went out to Attila the Hun to plead for the life of his Roman city. The legends tells us that Attila did not attack Rome because of two shining beings with flaming swords he saw on either side of the holy father.

Ascended Masters

The last type of guide I will discuss here is the Master teacher - spiritual beings from other time periods and planes of existence who choose, out of love, to return and share their wisdom with a mortal in the here and now. These are both men and women, and there are as many types as there have been cultures throughout the history of Earth. They run the gamut from Chinese herbalists, Mayan holy men, Aborigine trackers, Greek physicians, Tibetan lamas, Native American Holy men, Egyptian priests, and learned Rabbis from the past.

These guides are evolved, potent beings. They are members of the White Brotherhood, on this plane or another. Most have lived on Earth before and have a great commitment to serving humankind's spiritual upliftment. Whenever I meet one of them, I am shown a specific wisdom teaching he has to impart to the person whose life he is overseeing. Invariably, the initiate's interests become slanted toward that area of interest, although the person may not even realize he is being taught in the dream state.

Masters show up specifically to help with the actualization of a person's destiny. There are usually karmic ties between the teacher and student. And while the master has passed out of the reincarnational range of Earth's vibrational rate, the student is given the opportunity now in this life time to achieve his own mastership. The student's destiny may take the form of remembering healing methods ready to be brought back to the planet now. He may be activated to decipher ancient languages he has known in the past or to remember sacred geometry, vibrational science or some sort of spiritual wisdom forgotten in recent millennia. One's mission may have to do with uncovering ancient archaeological sites which are destined to be brought to light once again, helping to shift the consciousness of our world paradigm forward. Even as you read these words, I know that these activations are happening across the globe to many people. We are awakening to our true purposes.

If such Masters have chosen to enter your life, treat them as you would any sage of high regard. They are powerful, but they will not do the work for you. They will guide and nudge you, and as your life begins to unfold they will be there during times of need. They may stay throughout the course of your entire life, or they may pass you over to your next set of teachers once their work is done, even as the Vairagi did with me many long years ago.

Order Beneath the Chaos

In essence, this time of personal difficulty in my life taught me a great deal. I yearned to meet my next set of teachers, yet I was being guided to trust as the work I was doing for others unfolded. I learned that spiritual guidance often comes at our times of greatest darkness and doubt. At the leading edge of our discomfort, our sadness, our loss or our pain, or even our confusion is the opportunity for miraculous change. Such uncertainty allows these Divine messengers to step in and help if they are invited.

The Universe is far more vast than my limited human concepts had imagined, and even when I found myself confused, frightened and blind, I came to realize that I was never alone. The secret was in being still enough to "tune into the other frequencies" — a difficult task when you are under emotional and financial stress. As I beheld the presence of so many Loving beings, I realized that there was an order beneath the chaos that moved in the unfolding of our lives. Even when we could not see it, when we had nothing but our faith to help us through, Divine Order breathed Its breath upon us.

We could curl up into a ball and curse our lives. We could struggle and rage, deny and fume. We could close our inner hearing and inner sight and buy into this world of hardship, but in the end Spirit would still be there patiently waiting. And our Guides, our Guides would be right beside us, no matter what.

Who had set this plan of Grace in motion in the world? There are many names for It, and they are all ONE. I imagined this Supreme Benevolence coursing through the Universe, and I realized that millions of people do not even acknowledge it exists. Like a heartbeat, like the sound current I had heard as a child, like the pulse of love remembered and then forgotten, we have only to recall It, and It is there. God is everywhere: as nature, Muse, god or goddess, Angel, or animal. Even in the times when we are most blind, that Highest Love defies the vision of our mortal sight.

Life Stories

During these years of deep inner searching, I ached to meet my own angelic guides. I wanted to know who was guiding me behind the scenes, yet they had not appeared. Meanwhile I was being directed to help others through my readings. In these elegant, complex tapestries, I traced the roots of people's lives backward, discovering the octaves my gifts opened for me. I found I could read from photographs because silver holds the etheric imprint of a living field. I could follow soul mates through time, tracing relationships into the present. And I learned that the karmic bonds we build over time resonate in patterns that bring us together again and again for the sake of healing and love.

Wounds That Must Heal

One of the most important discoveries I made was that most of us have emotional issues which began centuries ago and are unresolved in the present. Many of these have been brought into this life with us. Since our Judeo-Christian paradigm doesn't embrace reincarnation, the roots of these wounds go unacknowledged and unhealed. During these marvelous readings I was allowed to trace unresolved issues in someone's life back to the *original trauma* - the place where it all began. Since the negative belief spun around the trauma was still in place, it operated to create the same self-limiting problems for the person again and again. These fears are like resurrected dragons we do not know how to kill. Until we heal them we will never be free.

With the grace of Angelic helpers, I found that I could dissolve the energy trapped in the sub-conscious mind and clear the beliefs. Being able to see how the injuries occurred was the key to understanding everything about our present lives. How different we all look when viewed from this perspective! So often what our mortal minds think about other people, has no bearing at all on who they really are. By seeing them through the eyes of true compassion, all subtleties are revealed, all wounds healed. These stories may aid you, or someone you know in identifying your own obstacles. Bear in mind as you read them that we are each unique. The same situation may have a dozen explanations when viewed from the perspective of soul's ultimate growth.

The Case of Sally

Sally was overweight, not merely by a few pounds, but by 150 pounds easily. Yet she had a lovely face and a gracious manner. I sat with her and her husband at dinner one night after a meeting, and they seemed like a happy, contented couple. They asked me if I would do a reading for them. I agreed. What turned up amazed me.

Sally had had a succession of lifetimes in which she had been so beautiful that wars had been fought over her. She had had to enter a nunnery or a temple in more than one lifetime merely to get away. Because of her intense physical beauty, Sally's life had been continually decided by one man or another for many centuries. Little opportunity had been allowed for the development of the usual mental or emotional pursuits. She had spent lifetime after lifetime being kidnapped, locked in towers, battled over, traded, married off, and taken in war. In short, she had been a pawn in someone else's list of desires.

In this lifetime Sally had chosen deliberately to be overweight. As a soul, she needed to develop other aspects of her spiritual, mental and emotional natures. Still pretty and attractive, Sally's apparent weight "problem" made this possible. It was a gift she was giving herself. In this lifetime, she and her overweight husband, Earl, had the deeply loving, safe relationship that allowed Sally to find a balance of all her needs.

The Case of Barbara

Barbara is a well-known stage actress in Los Angeles who is married to a famous male actor. I did a reading for her on one of my many trips out there. Theirs has been a tempestuous love affair from the start. While their relationship has brought them money, fame and happiness, it has also brought trauma, desperation and misery. Barbara was in a deep depression and seeking desperately for answers.

The sequence of lifetimes that showed up during Barbara's reading amazed me. A whole series of alternating lifetimes appeared, one after the other, following a specific pattern - male-female, male-female, etc. In each female lifetime, Barbara had been married to this same man. She appeared as innocent and submissive, always abdicating all responsibility and power to him to make decisions. He, in turn, became the dominator/controller. He would be unfaithful and then leave her feeling like a helpless victim.

Alternately, in her male lifetimes Barbara would incarnate as a brutalizing man, playing out the victimizer role in nefarious situations. She had been an Arab thief, a Jewish murderer, a Middle Eastern smuggler, etc. She's Jewish in this lifetime, so the bleedthroughs from that part of the world are still with her. Now I had never seen a soul pattern that had this kind of range to it before. It was most unusual. It became obvious that in this lifetime, Barbara's challenge is about finding a balance in her own inner male and female natures. She is learning about the balance of being neither the victim nor the victimizer. Needless to say, her husband's life path is intimately entwined with hers, and both of them are enmeshed in this same set of karmic lessons.

The Case of Ian

Ian is a quadriplegic. I met him at a seminar about spiritual growth. It was his first seminar of this type, but he seemed a bright, loving soul trapped inside a body without any freedom. His injuries were so severe that he could only move his wheelchair by blowing into a tube, yet he shared with me that the injury done to his spinal cord was actually repairable. Instead of being completely severed in his athletic injury, the accident had caused pressure to be placed on the spinal cord during an athletic injury. I could not even imagine what I would find when I went to read for him.

I took his hand and closed my eyes, praying for insight and guidance in this most difficult of readings. What turned up were two lifetimes as an Inquisitor during the Italian and French Inquisitions. He was brilliant and educated, a man high up in the political and religious orders. I saw scenes of people receiving visions and hearing voices, as if it was the time of Joan of Arc. Ian did not like such things. When these reports of healings, visions and so forth came in, he felt that if such a thing were possible that **he** should be the one to experience such miracles. After all **they** were just peasants! Did **he** not have the intelligence? Did **he** not have the proper aristocratic bloodlines? Certainly God would chose him before He would chose a mere peasant!

Without rational proof, Ian refused to believe in "a spiritual universe." I saw him railing to the skies, "If this is true, God, then let **me** have these visions!! Then I will let these people go free!" But as we all know, God doesn't come to the bargaining table like this. So Ian sentenced hundreds of people to death by torture and burning.

The spiritual perspective that most amazed me about this reading was realizing that Ian's quadriplegic status was not really a "punishment" for these acts, as one might naturally tend to think. In fact, it was an opportunity. For many lifetimes, Ian had had a well developed physical prowess as well as a great intellect. In this lifetime he was on his way to becoming an Olympic athlete when he had his accident. He had come to depend on these natural mental and physical abilities to the exclusion of his spiritual development.

Now, confined to a wheelchair in this lifetime, he has few choices. He could become a bitter old man or begin to explore those parts of his spiritual nature that he had ignored for so long. After his accident, Ian opened a school for young gymnasts with the accent on safety. He had already begun the work of being of service to others.

I was then shown a most peculiar vision. It was a vision of a steel room, a metaphor, I realized, for his mind. A door in this room was opening to the stars. I saw Ian's consciousness for the first time beginning to move out into the cosmos of the stars. Ironically, I remembered that the spiritual seminar he had been attending when I met him was on the science of "soul travel." I realized that Ian's quadriplegic condition was a gift he was giving himself for a temporary period of time. Since he was confined to the wheel chair, he had to rely on other methods of traveling. He was learning to leave his body and journey into the Inner Planes, and this finally would give him the wisdom he had sought for so long. Ian was perfectly on track with his life, even if from the worldly perspective, it didn't look like that to the mortal sight.

The Case of Alice

Alice is an artistic producer in advertising. She is a highly intelligent, sexy woman who desperately wants a romantic relationship yet avoids the opposite sex like the plague. In this lifetime, she has had a succession of emotionally and physically abusive relationships with men, at a personal and a business level. They have left her scared and frightened and wary of trusting herself. She is also a spiritual woman who attracts terrific people and situations with one hand, and continually finds herself in "victim/control" situations with the other. For years her throat has given her problems. She intuitively knows it has to do with her past life traumas.

During Alice's reading we were transported to a lifetime in the Ottoman Empire where, as a Princess to the Sultan, her entire life was controlled by men. First her father, and then her abusive warrior husband. She was told point blank that "her wishes were of no consequence to anyone." She was not allowed to ask for what she wanted. She was entirely made to "serve a man's pleasure."

These same beliefs have colored her intense desire to please men on one hand, and on the other have left her with total feelings of suffocation if she unites with one. After lifetimes of intense physical and psychological abuse that eventually resulted in her death, Alice came away with the belief, that "It is not okay to be myself. It is not okay to ask for what I want." Her throat problem is directly related to that underlying belief. She was, in fact, strangled to death by her warrior husband. Now Alice is beginning the process of positive affirmations and emotional clearing that will (hopefully) allow her to learn to stand up for herself and to ask for what she really wants.

The Case of Peter

A man named Alex came to see me. He was in great grief. His mentally retarded child, Peter, had suffocated in his crib two months earlier. Alex had been in the house at the time of the child's death, and he blamed himself for not preventing it. His wife blamed him as well, and the guilt he felt was now destroying his marriage.

During the reading an amazing thing happened. I was shown an image of a strong spiritual seeker who appeared in the body of a grown man. This adept had suffered through many lifetimes to at last attain a level of wisdom through much hardship. Yet, the one thing he lacked was the remembrance of pure joy and love. In my vision, the man stepped into an elevator and coalesced into a Being of light. Then he descended into this happy, beaming little boy who had been Alex's son, Peter.

Peter had deliberately chosen to be born mentally retarded because he did not want the burden of a strong mind again. What he needed most was to experience the pure healing that only unconditional love can bring. Alex and his wife were the perfect vehicles to give that kind of unadulterated feeling. As a baby, Peter had never intended to live more than a couple of years, yet the happiness he had experienced from his parents made him linger longer than he intended. He stayed until he was four years old.

During the course of my reading, Peter's spirit entered the room. It was an unprecedented event for me. I saw him clearly as the tall, handsome man he is in the spiritual kingdoms beyond. He knelt at his father's side and spoke words to him that only his father would understand. And as his father wept, Peter told Alex how much the love they had given him had meant. It had freed him as nothing else could have.

Not only did Alex received a profound healing that day, but I had received an enormous lesson about the complexities of human life. From the mortal perspective we often think we know what something is about. Why is someone born mentally retarded? Why are some born blind or deaf? It is easy to make judgments from our limited perspectives down here, but if we could but see from the higher vantage point, we would realize that the Universe is a far more complex and compassionate place than any of us have ever guessed.

In Summary

During these explorations of our own past lives, the most pertinent thing to remember is, "What have I learned in this life and what do I still fear learning? What are we learning today?" Uncovering the erroneous belief systems that have controlled our lives over and over, is the key to releasing ourselves from these self-imposed limitations and getting on with our happiness and growth. In the realm of emotional issues, recurrent karmic themes continue to repeat if we do not work them out. *There is no escape.*

By the same token, the gifts and abilities we acquire each lifetime are there, just below the surface of our conscious minds. No one we love is ever lost. Strong bonds like love, hate and loyalty will always pull us back into each other's lives again and again. Those with whom we feel an immediate resonance are usually people we have known and loved before. They are committed to helping us with our growth because they love us, just as we are committed to helping them. Those who evoke the opposite response may be relationships that were left in conflict, hurt and anger. *What we do not resolve in this lifetime will pull us back again and again to complete until we do so.*

As souls we are given many opportunities to develop our honesty, courage, focus, love, compassion, balance, and truth. Anything unresolved in one life rolls over to the next. We repeat the lesson until we get it right. WE REPEAT THE LESSON UNTIL WE GET IT RIGHT. And even after we get it right, we may still see it again ... just for practice.

Perhaps most importantly, during times of great personal struggle, upheaval or hardship, what appears from our point of view to be a handicap or a misery is often the opportunity to make a giant leap in consciousness. The Universe is giving us a chance to look at life in a completely new way. Always the leading edge of our pain, suffering and doubts will bring us to the precipice. If we will but make that leap, our entire lives will move into the next level of self-realization.

The Oracle Appears in Atlanta

 was Winter. I had agreed to videotape a PSI Conference that was happening here in Atlanta. Since I am by profession a commercial advertising photographer, I thought it was a way of contributing to the Psychical Research Society that might allow me to spend some quality time with some of the leading researchers in human consciousness. This three-day event included pioneers in out-of-body research, near death experiences, channeling and a host of other things. I knew some of them; others I did not.

One of my friends, Dr. Mark Woodhouse, a professor at Georgia State University, was helping host it and throughout the weekend he would say, "Tricia, there's someone here I want you to meet." Concurrently, I would pass this striking woman in the lobby and we would say, "Don't I know you?" "Yes, don't I know you? We have to talk." Of course, I later discovered that this was the very woman Mark had wanted me to meet. Her name was Nancy McCarey.

The last day of the conference, we finally found a few minutes to sit down on the couch in the lobby and talk. All I knew about her was that she lived in Hawaii and was very striking. Long blonde hair hung to her waist in a style reminiscent of an ancient goddess. Her wide set eyes were gray-blue, and her pert nose turned up.

As we sat down, I placed my hand over the back of the couch touching her hand. Because my clairvoyance is heightened through psychometric touch, I was instantly flooded with scenes from past lives we had lived together. In fact, the images were so strong that I could not concentrate on having a conversation. In quick succession they flashed by like scenes from an old movie.

Scenes From the Past

We were nuns serving in a Christian order in France about 899 AD. Nancy and I had worked side by side. We were Priestesses of Isis in ancient Egypt, healers and prophets for the upliftment of humankind. Last and most painfully was a lingering scene in ancient Crete of a wrenching death as the two of us clung to one another in a stone pit awaiting execution. I could feel that others had died before us, some tortured, some starved to death. I watched Greek soldiers above us walking on the gray stone wall of the pit. It was the Age of Aries. The advancing Patriarchy was already beginning to supplant the Earth teachings of the ancient sisterhood.

This patriarchal force eventually eradicated all of the Temples of the Goddess throughout Europe, killing thousands in an effort to destroy the teachings that had come before them. Later this same torture was applied to Jews and Christians. Then when the Holy Roman Catholic Church took over after the death of the Emperor Constantine in the 4th century AD, it persecuted all other teachings with the same cruel abandon it had received in the centuries before. During the height of the Middle Ages, this narrow way of thinking culminated in the extinction of five million women healers under the tyrannical auspices of the Inquisition. Thousands of teachers died as they refused to give up the secrets of the Oracular Temples they guarded. Nancy and I had been two of those murdered.

"Nancy," I mumbled hoarsely, "I'm ... I'm being flooded with images of us ... images from the past. I can't even concentrate on what you're saying."

"Oh," she nodded sadly, "I see them too. That lifetime of being tortured in Greece is particularly horrible. We had such a nasty ending."

I was flabbergasted. Throughout all the years of my readings, even people who claimed to "tune in" to what I saw could not track these lifetimes in detail with me.

"Yes, there were a couple of hundred of us there at the time," she said. "We were the ancient order of Sibyls, women who could see the future."

I had heard of the Oracles at Delphi where the inscription above the Temple read KNOW THYSELF.

"We were a powerful force for the Light," she smiled bravely, "and our teachings lasted until we were eventually destroyed by those who most coveted our secrets. I have met others who died with us on my travels."

I began to cry soundlessly. It was not a rational thing. I could not even explain it. The sorrow which swept through me was deep and abiding. Even now, I can only express it as a release of such soul rending pain that I could not hold back the tears.

"Cry," she whispered as we embraced. "Cry now. It is good to remember the pain. We are just beginning our work again. Thousands who have come to spread Light in other centuries are now beginning to wake up. We must remember who we are."

The Wound that Must Be Healed

Memories swept through me and the pictures unfurled. She had been one of the Hierophants and leaders. I had been another. There were easily another hundred and fifty who served beneath us. We spoke as Oracles in the Temples of Crete and trained others to awaken their natural psychic gifts. Pilgrims came from miles away to seek guidance from us, and our medical and teaching programs extended through villages and towns across the Mediterranean.

I saw grottos and gardens around the Temple complex. They were beautiful and well-tended. I saw pavilions and plazas where healing arts were taught, herbs gathered, medicines prepared. I saw villages where songs were sung and sacred circles gathered to commemorate astronomical conjunctions. I saw the blessings of crops and seasons. I saw peace and growth and prosperity. I saw baptisms of babies and chanting to speed the passage of one's soul to the next life at death. I saw scrying and divination for events great and small. I saw conscious telepathic connections with extra-terrestrials who had left the Earth but had sown their psychic DNA in the wombs of the Priestesses who had been our ancestors.

Then the vision changed. Men appeared. Men with armor and spears. They dragged the women screaming from their apartments. They speared them. They raped them. They threw the rest in stone pits to torture for their secrets. Much as centuries later the Holy Order of the Cathars would be burned out by a jealous, fearful Roman Pope.

I followed the vision back to the Temples, where below ground hidden tunnels led to holy relics kept by the Sisterhood. We were running. Nancy and I were fleeing through these underground halls. They catacombed beneath the buildings. We could feel the psychic cries of our sisters above us dying. What could we do?

The scene changed. We were caught. We clung to one another inside this pit of gray stones. A superstitious priest had told them that by swallowing a certain poison, we would be forced to give up the secrets of who we were. A truth serum he called it. They would then have the location of the holy relics. It was a lie. We knew the poison would kill us, but then they could never force us to tell. We would be dead and the knowledge would die with us. They forced it down our throats laughing. We clung to one another in the pit crying.

"Until our return, sister!" we promised each other with our last desperate breaths — "Until our return."

I was suddenly on the couch again, holding the hand of the woman who had been with me in the pit. I knew she could see the visions just as I had. We embraced silently. I could not stop crying. For a long moment we held the memory, then gratefully it began to fade.

"Nancy," I managed, "we have so much to say. Can't you stay in Atlanta for a few days?"

She smiled knowingly. "Oh, but I am staying for four weeks. I'm going to teach a class on Channeling."

I hugged her again, this time in joy. "I didn't know you channeled!"

"Yes, I channel a Greek Oracle named Pheobus. Didn't I tell you?"

A Greek Oracle!! My mind reeled. I was suddenly back in time five years before at the temple of the Greek Oracle where my teacher had taken me long ago. Had I heard her correctly? A Greek Oracle?

My dream was suddenly before me. This was more than mere coincidence. "Since I'm going to be teaching, sister, don't you think it's about time you got back to channeling?"

My world spun upside down. It was as if I was suspended beyond time. Everything faded as I moved perfectly above my body, connecting this moment with all the others that had led me here — a perfect strand of pearls in time. I knew this seed had been planted by my Higher Self eons ago, and this was the signal I had been waiting for from the Universe. Now I knew why I had been taken to the temple of the Greek Oracle. Well, I thought ironically, my Guides certainly knew what they were doing, even if I did not.

"Yes," I looked her straight in the eye. "I think it's time."

They Come as Angels

The Beloved Appears

 class was a four week one. Once a week we were to meet at a local book store. The first night, I was told, was to address our fears and teach us centering techniques. This would prepare us to meet our Guides. The second week we were to have direct contact, and the last two classes our Guides would speak through us in a process called "channeling".

I was very excited, and to be honest, I was also nervous. I had no idea what to expect, and as I entered the large open classroom, I was surprised to see thirty or forty people already waiting for the class to start. Wow! I had no idea that in a conservative southern city like Atlanta, so many people would be present. Yet that first Thursday evening, every fear instilled into me by my Episcopalian upbringing was rearing its head. I knew something big was about to happen, and my Ego was resisting it tooth and nail.

Over The Edge

On that first night we began by pursuing all the classic questions about discernment of spiritual energies, protecting one's self with White Light, attracting the highest vibrational guides and why mediumship was banned from traditional religion for so long. Let me say that these are important questions to ask yourself.

Mediumship was frowned upon for many years because most people who did it acted as "mediums" for the dead. This is a whole different thing from talking with higher dimensional beings like Angels, which is what many of the Biblical prophets of old were doing. Those who have passed to the other side are only slightly more aware than we are (if that), and rarely have the spiritual development to act as responsible mentors for anyone. To speak with them is one thing, but to let them inhabit your body is quite another. In addition there are lower astral entities who are mischievous and even evil, and no one needs to be wasting time with them. So traditional mediumship was frowned upon for some legitimate reasons. Continually giving up one's sense of self to lower astral entities is destructive and self-debilitating - the opposite of the kind of empowerment and enlightenment we seek.

Only by aligning oneself with the highest angelic frequencies of service can we ourselves grow forward into greater expansiveness and understanding. In my opinion it is imperative to work with beings who come from the White/Gold Light who are currently serving that Light with devotion. Since my background is a Christian one, I call in the Christ energies *before* I begin any inter-dimensional work. This is the first order of business when one is working on the inner planes. Set your intentions and protect your field, and then you can ask the Angels to align themselves with you.

For those who follow other teachers besides Christ, let me say this. There have been many great Masters who have walked this planet. I honor all of them. Sai Baba, Babaji, Yogananda, Krishna, Buddha, Rama, St. Francis and Ammachi all have tender places in my heart. But I can think of no higher vibration than Christ, for He was the messenger of *unconditional love*. And that is the vibration I work within.

Each of you must choose a master who resonates with your heart, for this is a private matter. I say only this: choose wisely.

Channeling

Channeling is a process of allowing yourself to drop deeply enough into your Theta/Delta brain that you connect with higher beings of Light. For some people they must go "unconscious" because they have not built a bridge between their Beta brain and their deeper connection to the Divine. For others, they remain present but submerged, as I do. They surrender their primary Ego to allow the Angelic frequencies to speak. These master energies usually live on fourth, fifth or even sixth dimensional levels. Most channels today are working with beings from the fifth and sixth density planes, places which are quite exquisite by any yardstick, and close enough to Earth's vibrational field to be able to help us in this time of transition. The fifth dimension is deeply involved with overseeing human life. They are still close enough to be able to help if they are asked. Many of the extra-terrestrials coming to visit Earth now live in the fourth and fifth dimensional levels, although occasionally a sixth dimensional race will appear. While many of these races know far more about what is happening with our galaxy and our solar system than we do, most of them still only have a part of the larger puzzle.

The Attitude of Gratitude

There is a secret to good channeling. It has to do with the correct alignment of the heart. No Light being can work through you except in accord with your own vibration. There must be a frequency match at some point of the continuum. They did not chose you randomly, and this is part of the unfolding process of discovery that happens as you enter into conscious relationship with them. The true purpose of any channeling is to create a partnership for our *individual upliftment*. It is not "to perform parlor tricks" for others, or even to answer psychic questions for an audience. It is to create a relationship between yourself and the higher realms that gives you direct access to inner wisdom. With this divine relationship, we begin to listen "within" for our answers, instead of placing empowerment outside of ourselves with a church, an institution or even a government.

To successfully contact these Higher realms we must begin with an "attitude of gratitude." Gratitude opens the heart. Begin by thinking of what you are grateful for in your life. Is it your health? Your friends? Your family? Your job? When we praise the abundance of God in our lives, it multiplies. This is the secret to entering the Higher realms. It is with our hearts that we open a path for Angels to meet us, and that is the beginning of learning to trust the "small still voice within".

Servants of the One

It is also important to remember that Guides are neither omnipotent gods nor demons. They are teachers, albeit Angelic ones. We may feel awe in their presence. We may feel tremendous love and even devotion, but we have no need to fear them or to worship them. That is not their proper role, and they would not be happy if we did. They too serve the Creator, and they would be the first to tell you we are all Divine beings in different stages of evolution.

Yet on that first night of my class, I was filled with all the apprehension that my strict religious upbringing had instilled in me. And I was torn between excitement and fear. Who would come? Who would my guides be? What if I didn't like them? What if my fundamentalist family was right, and monsters were lurking just around the next corner to take over my body? Scenes of the "Exorcist" rolled through my head. Looking back, I have to laugh at all the years of sub-conscious fear I carried around.

The Class Begins

After an hour or so of questions, Nancy instructed us to center ourselves and begin deep and rapid breathing. She led us into a slow, beautifully guided meditation to a place of safety. There, she instructed, we would begin to feel their presence with us. She did not want to rush. Around us I could sense the room filling with strong and loving lights. You could feel it in the air.

We were taken down a path by the sea shore. There the ocean swirled around our toes. Sea gulls flew overhead. Not another living human was in sight. From a distance we could sense a figure coming toward us. We knew it was our Spirit Guide.

Afterward the class talked about their experiences. Some had glimpsed a color or a figure. Others had seen a light. We would meet them next week, she told us. This was merely the invitation. Angels work through invitation, a rule of courtesy in the higher kingdoms. By opening up a dialogue, we create a space to communicate.

The Crystal Cave

The next week we returned, excited and nervous. This was the night we would actually learn their names. After so many years of waiting, I could hardly believe I was finally going to meet them! Within minutes we had lain down on the floor to do our first process. Again we were instructed to breathe in a particular manner, a pattern designed to take us deep within ourselves to the core of who we were. I found myself drifting back to the seashore we had visited the week before. Yet this time I saw a cave to one side of the beach line. I was immediately drawn toward it and found myself picking my way over the igneous rock and the foam, down, down into a large cave that was lit from within.

It gleamed with the shapes of frozen stalactites, crystalline formations of dazzling beauty. The color was a blue frost white. Light refractions glinted off the walls and ceiling, and the cave formed continuous arches above me. I could see my breath coming out in the frosty air, but for some reason I was not the least bit cold. I only knew that I was waiting — waiting for someone very dear to me to approach.

A stir began along the hairs of my arms. He was coming! I could feel it! The aura of this great Being approached, and I could hear the rustle of his cloak before my eyes ever glimpsed him.

Majestic! His eyes shone golden and brown like liquid light. He was tall and broad-shouldered, dressed in a tunic and long flowing cloak. Enormous wings spread behind him. His chest and arms were well muscled as he held them out to me. I took his hands. They were beautiful and well-shaped. At his shoulders were feathers of white and brown that rustled when he turned, and his head — it was the head of an Eagle!

"Beloved," the voice resonated inside my head. His hands closed upon mine. I stood transfixed. I knew this being! Majestic and regal, I looked into his eyes and beheld a vision beyond any I had ever seen in this world. He's an Eagle, I blinked in amazement, and the most incredible thing was that it seemed perfectly natural. Of course he was this way!

A feeling of indescribable love came over me.

"Yes, it is I." His voice was a reverberation within my head, and it was filled with the deepest gentleness I had ever heard. Rigel! Tears sprang to my eyes. I knew in that instant that he was the Being who had been with me all the heart-wrenching years of my childhood, the One who had walked with me invisibly, comforted me in the darkness and given me counsel. He was the one who had said of the Vairagi, "This is the path I have placed you on, Beloved. Follow it."

I recognized him as I would recognize the essence of all that I was. I bit back the sob in my throat. Rigel! I had looked for him throughout all my years of study with the masters, all the prayers by my altar ... and I had despaired of ever finding him again. I could barely see for crying. After so long, so much heart-rending pain, how could he be here with me again?

Rigel! His presence filled me and I knew that he was reading every feeling that I had. I knew his vibration as I would know that of my mother or my father. Yet he had never let me see his face until now. It had eluded my inner vision. Even with my gifts of clairvoyance, he had never permitted me more than a glimpse of his strong, tall body until today.

Rigel ... the years of my childhood spun by me. When I was younger I had raged at him in anger, "Just show yourself! Just materialize!" Now I realized why he had kept this from my vision. I was too young to know this secret.

"We have much to say, you and I." The words were a warmth that pulsed out to my whole body. It was the glow of healing. "All that is important now is for you to know that I am here with you, and I will not be leaving you again." A fresh wave of tears caught me. He smiled as tenderly as any father. I had not realized how alone I felt in the world until that moment. "I have never left you, Beloved. I know it is hard to believe, but our meeting has been predestined for this time. You had much to do before you were ready to see me for who I am." I felt the truth behind his words, and despite my tears, I could not look away.

To my left the shimmer of another energy began. Something was materializing in the cave. Rigel turned in respect. I turned with him. It was a gossamer movement of translucence. She began to coalesce into the shape of a fairy ... or was it an Angel? The presence of a female being of great joy, lightness and love surrounded us, but she did not become stable to my vision. She remained a moving flutter of rose and amethyst lights. Even when I tried to see her face, she was more impression than solid, more movement than definition —a swirling dance of light and color.

This beautiful energy bowed. "I am Auriel. I bid you greetings."

The voice was music itself. Love emanated from her like a song. Auriel ... was that spelled with an O or an A? She laughed.

"I spell it with an O, but you may speak it with an A. A is the beginning, and O is the center, and I am both of those things." I smiled and bowed back at her. She was a Being of such delightful joy that her presence settled over me like the glow of a magic lantern on a warm summer's night.

"Are you an Angel?" I asked her.

She laughed and the sound was like chimes in the wind. "You could say that I am. I am a being of the heart, and I live within the center of your galaxy and beyond. I am present for all people and all races. You may call me Auriel of the Council of Nine." Her colors danced through the cave. Exquisite!

How could these teachers be mine? I was dazzled. They were breathtaking! They were beyond anything that I had imagined, yet I knew them as one knows a family member one has not seen for a very long time. They were part of my blood, my very being, unnamed until today, eternal in my heart.

Celestial Words

Behind me in the room, I could hear Nancy signaling our return back to the physical world. I was not ready to go. Rigel heard my thoughts. "It will be fine," he nodded regally. "We are not leaving. We go with you whereever you go."

"Allow yourself to become aware of your body in this room. Allow your awareness to shift back to this time and this place." It was Nancy's voice.

My breath tightened in my lungs. I could not leave after just finding them again, but her voice was calling us back through the tunnel of lights. I was becoming less substantial. The cave started fading around me. "Not yet! not yet!" I cried, but Nancy's voice spoke across the distance of dimensions.

"Pick up the pencil beside you on the floor and start to write. Let your Guides speak to you in a letter. If you listen closely, you will hear what they are saying." I felt my body back in the class room, but I did not open my eyes. My hand picked up a pencil and found the paper that was lying by my elbow. I had never done this before. I did not even know if I believed in "automatic writing." I opened my eyes and then shut them again. In my head I could still hear Rigel speaking.

"Go ahead, you can do it." I put one hand over my eyes, put my pen to paper and began to write the words that he was speaking.

"Beloved,

You wonder who I am. I have been known by many names throughout many ages. In ancient Egypt I was called Horus, yet I have incarnated on a thousand worlds and I am known across all galaxies. You see me as a god, yet I walk among you as a man. I live in a place where many that you would call gods have existence. Yet I am but a servant of the ETERNAL ONE. I am Truth. I am justice and clear vision. I am the wings that span across the Infinity of space. I know of the illusions of Time/Space and electro-magnetic fields, for I help to regulate them. Through my spiral I move everything into creation. I am He who stands beside you as your father. I have been with you throughout the ages and I will not leave you now. Do not weep, my daughter. We shall not be parted again.

Rigel"

Huge tears weld up inside my eyes, and I had to hold my breath not to sob aloud. His love was more profound than any I had ever known. Though he was an enigma, I knew his words were true. Who was he though, my mind asked. And how had we been joined before? Had he been my father, teacher, mentor in some higher dimensional plane? Had I somehow forgotten him? It seemed impossible, and yet it was the only explanation. How patient these timeless beings were! I realized that they would wait for us through millennia. I put my head down on the page and felt hot tears roll down it. The pain of recognition was breaking me. It was almost more than I could bear. What love they bore us, and what ceaseless patience!

Auriel moved into my field then, and her words spoke softly in my head. "Do not cry, beloved one. We are with you now. The long, hard struggle is over, and you can rest."

This only made me cry harder. Did everyone feel this depth of sadness and release at the coming of their guides? They had placed their finger on some spring inside my heart, and I was caught in remembering some emotion I could not even name. I felt indescribably homesick, like I had been gone so long I had forgotten where I came from. I had not even realized how alone I'd felt. Now that they had come ... Why, I had waited for this all of my life.

"Who are you really?" I asked silently. She smiled.

"I am Auriel. I am the Mother and Heart of all things. I forgive all things. I heal all things. I know all sadness and all fear. Nothing is too dark for me to love it into wholeness. Nothing is too hidden that I cannot find and mend it. I am the Mother of Creation, as Rigel is the Father. Throughout all of the ages, it is to me that the people of all worlds have turned to rest in the bosom of my heart."

My heart ached within me, a burning physical hurt, yet the murmur of her sweetness began to lift the pain. She heard my unspoken question . "Are you the mother Mary?" I had followed Mary's numerous appearances in different countries around the world, and always felt great love for her.

"I am the matrix from which all Divine Mothers spring. Each of them is contained within me, as I indwell them. All may rest in the bosom of who I am. Be joyous and at peace, my dearest child. There is no true aloneness in the world, save that of ignorance. In your "not knowing," you believe yourself to be alone. Yet we are with each of you and we love you with all our hearts."

I don't know how long I lay there, letting the feeling soak in. The pain began to melt. She had placed a hand over my deepest grief and lifted it for the first time. After a long time, Nancy asked us to let our thoughts return to the room, and slowly, oh so slowly, I came back, clutching my precious letters in my hand as they were the only tangible evidence of this new reality.

To Change Your Life

Now, the group of forty or so people began to share. No two stories were alike, yet each had seen two guides: one male, one female. People reported beings with names as common as Joe, Mary or Frank. Others were exotic. Some were Angels, farmers, holy men from the Bible. Some appeared as Eastern wise men, Native American Shaman, wise women, devas, or extra-terrestrials. Some were as old as grandfathers, others younger than the people they guided. To my logical mind there seemed no specific pattern, except that each person was *profoundly altered* by the transmissions that had passed between them. Their faces were lit from within and their voices were softly awed.

I cannot adequately describe the wonder of a meeting such as this. It is profoundly life changing. Imagine if you will, that you have had amnesia all of your life. Then one day you suddenly come to your senses. You awaken from a fog of absolute forgetfulness. And who should greet you but your long lost friend and companion, a Divine, loving being who has been sitting by your bedside throughout your long convalescence, a being who has waited and prayed for your return to consciousness.

Meeting one's Guides is the most profound experience of a lifetime, and my wish for each of us on this planet is that we awaken to such a joyous remembrance in this life time.

We Like the Miracles

 next two weeks were full of miracles. For years I have worked with UFO investigations, and I head up a large group called the UFO FORUM in Atlanta. Once a month we bring in a credible, national speaker for the general public to inform the general public as to what is going on world-wide with the UFO situation. We have had Colonels from the military, psychologists, ex-NASA people, physicists, astronomers, and even abductees. Our speaker on this particular month was Dr. Steven Greer, an emergency medical physician from Asheville, North Carolina. He had come to speak about telepathic techniques he had developed for contacting extra-terrestrials.

Dr. Greer arrived on the Friday night following the channeling class and spoke. The next day he held a seminar, and we led a group of fifty or so people northward to camp in the North Georgia Mountains. The place was called Black Rock Mountain State Park, and our sole intent was to try to "call in" some physical space ships.

It was a wonderful gathering of people, many who were established professionals in the community and who had become curious about the UFO phenomena. Some had even had their own UFO sightings in the past, as I had. We were purposefully involved in a process called CE-5 or Close Encounters of the Fifth Kind, which uses a type of mental telepathy to make contact. The premise is that if a space ship is within range, the telepathic beings on it will "hear" the signal if we have enough focused mind-power. Dr. Greer has had considerable success in the past, and has video tapes to prove it. I have repeated these same procedures myself with various groups in Florida, Nevada, California, Peru and England and called in space ships each time.

This was the first time I had gone through the process though, and we were all very excited. We got centered, made the "call" and had five or six lights appear above us in the sky for about thirty minutes. It was exhilarating! They hovered soundlessly, jumping in space and making loops. We all stayed up well past 3:00 a.m., finally sleeping on blankets on the cold, hard ground.

Sunday dawned. I awoke with a sharp crick in my neck and shoulder, which rapidly became excruciating. It grew steadily worse as the day progressed, and on Monday morning I went to the chiropractor. The pain did not improve. I returned on Tuesday and Wednesday, by this time in such pain that I could hardly work. This had never happened before. My chiropractic visits number around a dozen a year, so needless to say, I was irritable and at my wits end to get rid of it.

The Class Reconvenes

On Thursday night our channeling class reconvened. Even though the pain had gotten steadily worse, I was not going to miss this class. It was to be the first night that we voice-channeled, and we were all excited and nervous. After about thirty minutes we broke into groups of two, deliberately choosing partners we knew nothing about.

We sat facing each other, knee to knee, and began our breathing exercises. The breath does many things, including centering one's energy. It also opens up energetic pathways to heighten one's senses. Wise people from the East have long called it the Prana, or life force, and it is used in everything from Yoga to athletic conditioning, from preparation for singers to public speakers. I strongly recommend such breathing exercises for all sorts of spiritual, physical and meditative work.

During the week I had felt the bond with Rigel humming. It was strong, and I had no doubt he would show up, but I was apprehensive as well. He is powerful, and it is sort of like realizing you are a hundred watt light bulb and have a 10,000 watt voltage coming to visit. A little intimidating at best.

Our instructions with our partner were to be guides for the other person as they channeled, and then allow them to act as guides for us when it was our turn. To this end we were encouraged to ask for messages that might come through our partner from his Guide or ours. We chose strangers because obviously if you knew a lot about your partner, it would be easy to pull from our own stock of mental information instead of trusting our Guides.

Trusting the Flow

Justin Oberman sat across from me. He was a tall, lanky fellow with oversized hands and a kindly face. I helped him through his process and greeted his Guide in the most cordial of manners. I asked his Guide if he had any messages for Justin. He did. Then I asked if he had any messages for me. He commented on my life, and although he was not very specific in details, he was accurate in what he said. A few minutes later, Justin returned to full consciousness and it was my turn.

I began my breathing induction process, and within a few minutes I could clearly feel the gentle presence of a Being settle across my shoulders. It was Auriel. I was surprised, for I had felt my contact with Rigel was stronger, and I had had no doubt that he would come.

Let me say that the experience of being a conscious channel is quite different from being an unconscious one. You do not simply "leave" the body. You are present and aware of everything. You are simultaneously experiencing *their* energy field as well as your own. You are hearing *their* thoughts in your head, as well as your own thoughts, and the thoughts are *very* different. The challenge is to allow yourself to surrender enough to let their identity become the dominant one, instead of your own; to step aside enough to allow their thoughts to be spoken instead of yours; to *surrender to the presence of who they are,_knowing your identity will not be lost.* This is a tough job for those of us who have Egos.

Auriel sat lightly in my body, only going down into my throat chakra, then slowly settling into my heart.   A sense of profound peace came upon me, mixed with a lyrical laughter. I could feel the joy of her, but I did not know how to share it aloud. It was as if I was in the Presence of dancing music, yet I had no words to communicate this feeling. Another part of me was in complete panic with just the thought that I would let anyone speak through me.

"Welcome," Justin greeted her.

"I thank you for your welcome," she answered graciously, and bowed to him.

That's not so bad, I thought inside myself. In fact it even seemed effortless.

"I am Auriel, and I greet you in the name of the Council of Nine. Do not be surprised that I have come instead of Rigel. We know of Tricia's fears and we are here to make things easier."

She did? She does? Is she talking about me?

"She has great concerns about letting go. It will get easier. We promise. We know that she is very gifted in this work, but lifetimes of being killed for communing with Angelic Beings such as ourselves makes it difficult for her to trust this process again."

"Where do you come from?" asked Justin.

"The essence of who I truly am is from the center of Creation, but in this meeting, I am blended with one from the star system Arcturus, so that I might more easily communicate with you. Arcturians are by nature healers who exist at a fifth and sixth dimensional vibration rate. This One I blend with is one of a number of Beings who work in the Angelic Realms and who are now in service to helping others in the healing of their own emotional bodies. In the beginning of such a contact as this, Arcturians are often chosen because they are so gentle. Suffice it at this time to say that our essence is One with the Christ and the heart. Our purpose is to serve the good of all humanity."

"Do you have a message for me?" Justin asked. This was part of what we had agreed upon before we started.

"Yes, you are like a tree, Justin. You are best when you are still, with your roots deep and your branches wide. Many will come to lay beneath your branches, for you are a healer. But remember that the truest healing comes from the vibration that emanates from your own Beingness."

"It is true," he nodded, "I am a healer and I love plants. I have been having problems lately. Can you give me some insight on those?"

"Indeed. Your problems stem from scattering your energies in too many directions at once. This is linked to an issue of self worth. Many on your world have this same issue, for it is taught to you as part of your world paradigm. Each person has his or her own way of coping with this lack of self love. Scattering your attentions to many people, so that you get external validation, is the method you have adopted in order to cope with this pain. But it does not ultimately serve you, for you over-extend and then disappoint others, getting as much criticism as praise."

"What should I do then?" he asked emotionally.

"Stop and love yourself. The reassurance you seek is in self-knowing, and self-love, not in the strokes of others. That will flow naturally when you are truly present for yourself. This self-love is what will give you inner peace."

He bowed his head. "Thank you, Auriel. All you have said is true. I will strive to do what you suggest." He took a deep breath, and I wondered what would come next. "You have a message for Tricia?"

"Yes we do. We know that she has a strong rational mind, and thus she is one who needs proof to know that what she has experienced is real. It is the voice of her father, the lawyer, speaking within her. We say to her that it is all right to doubt. It is all right to be afraid. It is merely a stage in the passing of the shadows across the illumination of the moon. What is Truth does not die. It can be tested and its worth can be proven over time. As the flower unfolds, so does each of you humans. Allow yourselves to be afraid but to step through your fears to the other side. All sorts of miracles await you there, and we know she likes miracles."

"Thank you," Justin said. I could feel the sweet kiss of her energy beginning to move out of my chest. I felt a love from her so strong and so gentle that I knew she had come because I had been so afraid. Her angelic feminine energy was exactly what I needed. I prepared to return to full consciousness.

Suddenly Rigel's presence was immediate. He stepped inside my chest and a deep masculine voice spoke. "Hold! I come but for a moment. I am Rigel and I come to tell her she is loved. Only this. Justin, repeat these words to her: Say to her that I will not leave her again."

A sense of power, and devotion such as I had never known swept through me. "Will not leave her .... " the words reverberated. How often I had despaired that all my faith in God's love was theoretical, that there was no personal love from an Infinite Creative

Source. How often I had wondered whether anyone in the Heavenly realms even knew I existed. Now, these beings had proved that
I was wrong. God's love is personal and it works through the presence of beings such as these. They are the doorways to remembering who we are, and knowing that what transpires on this world can
be guided from the next.

Miracles

When we returned to the circle of the class and shared what
we had seen, Nancy reported what she saw around me clairvoy-
antly. Auriel's energy was seen as pink with geometric shapes, something I have since learned that many Arcturian's appear to be. Pink
is the color of the heart, the color of love. Nancy had not seen
Rigel's brief appearance.

This description of Auriel has changed somewhat over the years,
for as I began to link more and more directly with her, the presence
of the geometric Arcturian was no longer needed. Now people feel
or see her descend into the room as a beautiful glowing heart of
rose light. She has said that the pink rose is the fragrance most akin
to her essence, and that smelling it opens the heart of the receiver.

Rigel is usually described as a brilliant column of white light.
People see him descend over me towering up through the ceiling.
Occasionally they will see wings, or a hawk or eagle's head behind
me, but whether one sees or not, his presence is always felt. His
motion is perceived as a moving spiral of stars turning like the inside
of a galaxy ... but I get ahead of myself now.

The morning after this class was the real miracle. I awoke completely free of pain! After five days of continuous torture, my neck
was suddenly and miraculously healed! And now I understood why
Auriel had said in her beautiful, melodious voice, "Tricia likes the
miracles."

Keeping the Flame Alive

In the week that followed, their energy stayed with me like a shield of loving protection. I could hardly wait until the night of the last class. We were paired up with another "stranger" to allow a maximum freedom of experience. I was with a girl named Julia. I was nervous, but this time I was ready to let Rigel speak. He came through immediately, and his first words caused a ripple of shock to go through me.

"It is good to see you again, Julia." What could he possibly mean? How had *my* guide met her before?

Julia was equally uncertain. She answered hesitantly. "Have we met before?"

"Indeed, you were only thirteen years old when I came as a column of light to your bedroom one night. It was summer. I know you remember. It was from that point on that you began to seek spiritual wisdom. Is this not true?"

The girl was flabbergasted. "Ye..s..s ..."

What the hell was happening? How had *my Guide* come to someone else? I could feel Rigel's amusement at my dilemma. "Pay attention," he said silently, "and you will learn."

"I thought it was only a dream," Julia whispered in awe. "I thought that God had visited me. And after that .... I began to look for Him everywhere."

"In a manner of speaking, God did visit you. Am I not a servant of the One? The Infinite is not only vast, it is personal as well, Julia. Since I am here now, I know there are questions you wish to ask.

Go ahead and begin."

Julia hesitated. "I ... I don't want to be silly, but what can you tell me about this relationship I'm in? What should I do about it?"

Much to my astonishment, Rigel went on to advise her that she was in a relationship in which she gave her power away. "It does not support your spiritual growth or self-worth. You have repeated this pattern in many of your relationships, and it is only now that you are getting clear enough about this to change the pattern."

She nodded. He advised her to take a good look at why she constantly chose this in her mates, and to realize that she could choose a mate who supported her inner growth as well as her outer.

"Do you have a message for Tricia?" Julia asked when he was finished.

"It is this. If she would have a conscious relationship with us, she must take the time to cultivate it. So often the pace of the life you have been taught to lead in this civilization is rush, rush, rush. You struggle for money. You struggle for jobs. You struggle for time to create a relationship with yourselves, and that is usually at the bottom of the list. We are present with each of you all the time. We may appear in an instant if we are invited. But to build any meaningful dialogue, one must take the time to listen. Our message to her is one I send to each of you. Then you will have the answers you seek."

When I came out of this channeling experience, I felt very happy, even though I had been admonished for all the things I put in the way of my spiritual development. Rigel was right. I often procrastinated creating "alone time." I wanted to know immediately whether his insight on Julia's relationships were true. After all, I knew nothing about her, and here Rigel was telling her to basically choose another boyfriend.

Julia laughed. "It's the very crux of my relationship problems," she confessed. "I've suspected it all along, but I wasn't ready to face it ... until now. Thank you ... I mean thank Rigel for being clear enough to say it."

The class pulled its chairs into a circle to share. Nancy turned to me. "Tricia, you were channeling a different energy tonight. This was a strong column of white light that descended over you. I could see it clearly. There are many who wish to speak through you, angels and extra-terrestrials alike. Select one or two to hold the gate until you have grown stronger. Too many energies at once will only confuse you."

I nodded, knowing she was right. There was no question who the Gatekeepers would be — Rigel and Auriel. They were as dear as my own parents ... and infinitely more vast.

Lessons From the Front

The class ended that night. We all hugged and kissed goodbye, realizing that the challenge would be to keep alive our newfound experience and not to go back to the oblivion of forgetfulness. In the months that followed I tried to remember this. To that end, I began taking time each morning to write to my guides. This was hard to do.

Those of you who have tried it know what I mean. The phone rings. Your clients want you. You have to mail your bills. The world outside calls. It is hit and miss. Sometimes I could not still my mind. Sometimes I would just stare longingly at my meditation room, and promise to do better as I fled out the door to some crisis or another. Rigel's comments about my not taking the time to cultivate my relationship with my guides rang like a prophecy.

But several of us from the class had gotten together and started a support group. Every two weeks we faithfully channeled for one another. My guides often came out to speak to others, but usually their strongest advice was for me, their semi-delinquent student.

During these first few months of "partnership" they directed me in specific ways. First they told me to prepare to teach others. When I protested that I was not ready they said simply, "One step at a time, one foot in front of another. We ask no more than this."

Next they instructed me to consider hypnosis as a way of retrieving memories from my childhood I had always wondered about. These were dreams of UFOs, dreams of being on board space ships and talking with higher dimensional beings, and dreams of learning sacred geometry about the nature of the Universe. This opened up a whole new avenue for me, suddenly allowing me to make sense of personal experiences that created a bridge between the ET phenomena and the Angelic kingdom. I began to see how at the higher octaves, those we call Angels work hand in hand with the more advanced vibrational races.

Last, they told me to rent a hall in Los Angeles, pay for a plane ticket, buy a large ad in a Los Angeles newspaper and teach a weekend seminar on what I knew. Looking back I think I must have been crazy to have taken on such a wild and expensive venture, but at the time, Spirit sent in exactly the right amount of money I needed to manifest this adventure. So I followed their advice and did so. Little did I realize that it would lead to my traveling worldwide and speaking to thousands of people.

The Dream

One morning I awoke from a prophetic dream. It was so strong that I was compelled to write it down. "What does it mean?" I wrote in my journal.

"Tell it to us, and we shall see."

I reconstructed it piece by piece. I had been traveling. I was going to speak to a huge audience. In fact, I realized with shock as I wrote it down, I was going to channel Rigel! But though I found this overwhelming in retrospect, it seemed neither unusual or scary in the dream. On the way to the hall someone asked a question about transformation. I stopped and drew a design for them. It was a cross with a large circle around it, like a Celtic cross. Four neat, perfect circles were inset into the design, one appearing in each of the four quadrants.

"What does this mean?" the person in the dream asked me.

"I don't know," I answered. "We'll have to ask Rigel."

I sat back in my meditation chair. "That's all I remember," I said aloud. "Can you please tell me the significance of this dream?"

Just then the phone rang. It was business. Three more calls followed it, and before I realized it, I was once again caught up in the day to day world of "doing." I had totally failed to get any clarity with my dream. I saw then that this pattern of constant distraction was more than my external circumstances. Part of it was within me. I could have left the answering machine on, but I couldn't say no. In frustration, I unplugged the phone and sat down, feeling disconnected from myself. I closed my eyes and asked for help.

Immediately Rigel's presence filled the room. "Why am I like this?" I asked him furiously. "Why do I avoid connecting with the Source when all I have to do is shut the world out for a few minutes?"

"It is because you dread the time of silence, Beloved." His voice was like a balm on my spirit.

"But why ... why?" I shouted.

"You dread it for many reasons. First you have been taught by your culture to avoid listening to yourself. You have your television sets, your radios, your cellular phones, all broadcasting such static that you can barely have a moment of peace. This keeps you in Beta Brain, that place of inner noise where the mind moves in constant circles but is never fulfilled."

I knew that place well. It was the very essence of the business work place, the discotheques and the television commercials that blared out at me whenever I turned on the set. In fact the news itself seemed to be full of the same negativity. Stories of rape, murder, car accidents and shootings filled our lives. How could anyone concentrate on inner peace or world harmony when we were addicted to this? No, it was designed to pull us away from the focus of the inner spirit.

"Why do we buy into it so easily?" I asked him. Perfectly good people get sucked into this madness every day.

"It is the Ego's fear of annihilation. The Ego knows that it is not the Spirit, but only a shadow of your true essence. The Ego knows that it is but a servant and that it has had the run of the house, which is yourself, as if it were the master. We tell you this, Beloved: That whatever your Ego wants, it shall have as long as you run from the place of silence within yourself. What you remember, and your Ego would like you to forget, is that in this moment of inner knowing is the real place of sanctuary. This is the place of power where all things are felt and known and experienced — not in the illusion of the material world."

"I know that, yet I forget ... " I said in exasperation. I took a breath.

The spiral of Rigel's beingness moved through me, and I felt myself extending my perceptions as if I stood at the center of a galaxy. This was his normal state of being. It was the center of all things. "I love this feeling," I whispered. "I love feeling connected to God, yet I run away. I don't know why!"

"Why do you run, Beloved? Because your Ego is afraid of dying. Because the Ego exists only through the illusion of separation from God, and when you are truly connected to God, the Ego has no power in your life."

I felt my heart melting. The swirl of stars around me seemed to brighten. Who was this majestic being who sat at the center of the galaxy?

"I am the still point at the heart of Eternity."

I felt a different motion now, as if I stood in the middle of a fountain of Light. Above us millions of photons like liquid life sprayed out into the heavens. They moved out into the Lower Worlds forming the solar systems, the suns, the people, plants and animals. Below us these same beings returned from their worldly excursions and within the presence of the being that He was, they passed again and again through the eye of the needle to be reborn into existence.

"Is this the Fountain of Life?" I asked silently. He smiled.

"It is the place that all must pass through to be born into manifestation. It is the Eye of Horus."

I had heard of the Eye of Horus, but I did not really know what it was. From my perspective it looked like the eye of the needle through which all things were recycled to live again. The roaring of light particles, souls in the river of time, coursed through my ears like a celestial river. I do not know how long I was gone before I heard beneath its current the melody of his words again.

"Do you not know that I am the answer to your hopes, your dreams, and your memories? I am the place where the cool lapping of water is felt on every pore of your being. I am the soft grasses and the swaying breeze. Here, here in this place of sanctuary, this place of utter stillness and movement, I bring you as I have brought countless others. Did I not bring the psalmist David to this same place when he wrote these words:

"The Lord is my shepherd, I shall not want.
He maketh me to lie down in green pastures;
He leadth me beside the still waters.
He restoreth my soul."

"That is my purpose and my being, Beloved - to restore the soul to its remembrance of itself. And that is the purpose of every divine being you would call Angel."

I felt a great sadness well up inside of me. I was such a delinquent beside this Being. I was impatient, distracted and undisciplined. Large self-indulgent tears rolled down my cheeks. "How can I speak to others of such a place? How can I describe the indescribable? I ... I don't think I can do it."

"Why?" he asked as gently as a father. I couldn't say the words, but Rigel heard them all the same.

"Ah! Because you are not worthy." A long, excruciating silence hung between us. I sighed. "That is the cry of the little self, dear one. Do you not yet see that we are all entwined, that every mote, every photon has my spark, and thus each one of you is Divine?"

"But why ... why have you picked me?"

His voice softened. "We will tell you. It is because you are a perfect example of the human condition."

Was he making fun of me? What did he mean?

He said with the utmost compassion. "You are the human condition, Beloved. You are the voice of distraction. You are the Egoic condition. You are the joy and the shadow. You are the shadow and the laughter. You are the sadness and pain. You are forgiveness and compassion. You are the perfect bridge to your people. You are Holy and you are full of holes."

I had to laugh at that one. It was so true!

His presence enfolded me like wings. "You are my Beloved. An

Infinite Being of Infinite Light. You are one to whom I am totally committed. You are my child and my mirror. I am your sanctuary. You are my Pilgrim. Have you not seen this yet?" I wiped my face with my sleeve. "Do not be so afraid. We are with you. Let go and allow us to move in your life."

"Can you tell me what my dream means?" I asked him. "Can you tell me what the symbol meant? It was a cross within a circle."

The Shadow of Things To Come

"Ah, those are the four initiations you will go through in your learning - fire, water, earth and air. And when you have completed them, you will truly stand in the circle of yourself."

"But what are they? What do they look like?"

"We will tell you when the time comes."

Lessons of the Heart

 flew to Los Angeles a month later, and people showed up at the workshop. Wonderful people. Lovely people. People who had had their own stirrings from Angels. One stood up and announced, "I have hosted a radio show for over four years, and you are the most balanced speaker I have ever heard on the UFO phenomena. When you talk, all the scientific and historical things begin to connect with the spiritual realms. You must start speaking nationally."

Two other people came up on break. "We want to buy your book. Where is it?"

"I don't have a book," I answered.

"But you must! We saw it in a vision before we ever came to your seminar."

I laughed. "Well, did you get the title?"

Suddenly I heard clearly in my mind. "Beings of Light, Worlds in Transition." Wow!! What a great title! I laughed. "Never mind, I think I just got the title. I'll let you know when it's finished."

Getting To Be Human

When I returned home I announced to Rigel and Auriel. "Okay, I'm ready. Send me the book." I could hear them chuckling. Somehow I had imagined they would reveal to me the entire history of the human race - maybe even the Galaxy - in a few easy sittings. UFOs, Angels, it would be simple. But my teachers were far more concerned with *my spiritual progress*, with the breaking free of *my lim-*

ited belief systems on planet Earth than they were with any discourses on space ships. Later, much later, that type of information did begin to come, but more than a year their focus was totally on the limits we humans place upon ourselves.

The Human Guinea Pig

Learning in this way was challenging. I would find myself placed in uncomfortable life situations set up to trigger certain emotional responses. Some of these feelings I had never experienced, or I thought I had mastered long ago. They ran the gamut from anger to jealousy, envy to fear, confusion, pain, frustration, guilt — you name it. If I sat down and immediately took a discourse the feelings would dissolve. But if I tried to figure it out for myself, as I usually did, the feelings grew stronger. After I had exhausted all of my efforts on whatever the "issue du jour" was, I would finally surrender, sit in silence and take a discourse. Immediately, everything became crystal clear. The emotional clouds passed and I would be left with a profound discourse on the nature of reality!

After a few months I figured out what they were doing. I had become the guinea pig for the entire human condition! It was a very annoying state of affairs! I was being allowed to go through countless human emotions in order to address them. "This is a lot of work!" I complained to them one day.

They laughed. "How can we teach you solutions to mankind's dilemmas if you have not experienced them firsthand? Do you not realize that in order to learn true healing you must first know what it is to be wounded? Real healing comes from the inside out, not the outside in. How can you hope to speak to humans as a teacher if you have not fully claimed your own humanity?"

"But it's all so emotional!!" I complained.

"That is the richness of the human condition. It is the bed of compost in which the crops of compassion are grown. You do not realize how many souls wish to be embodied just to learn what it is to feel as you feel now."

"But these feelings are so painful!"

"Feelings are the fuel which drives the motor of your desire. One may set one's will but it is one's true heart, which, when opened, pulls you to the Light of integration."

Foreshadowing The Shadow

I received discourses of fear, love, anger, blame, guilt, sex, relationships, freedom and responsibility, and in particular, my personal favorite, the Shadow. I could write an entire book on the Shadow (and perhaps I will) simply because it is so present and tenacious in our lives.

The Shadow is another way of speaking of the Ego, that little self which lives within us all and likes to think it is running the show. Nothing that I had ever done had ever made me so aware of the persistent, insidious presence of the Ego inside of me, as did my relationship with these beings. I was face to face with my Ego every day. Learning to surrender to these beloved teachers brought me to the mirror of my own fears and resistance in a way that nothing else had. I realized that no matter how much work I thought I had done in the past, I had much, much further to go

Going National

The phone rang a month later. It was my friend Dee Riggs. She was the one with the radio show who now worked as a sales director for a national company that produced seminars on consciousness. "I'm trying to get it arranged," she began. "I'm only a sales rep, but I really believe in what you shared with us, so I'm trying to arrange it so that you'll be invited to speak at our Expos next year."

My head spun. What kind of Expos? Who else would be there? How many people attended?

"We are in seven cities a year. Twenty to thirty thousand people come to each one, and we hope to expand to another five cities soon."

I swallowed hard. "Who speaks at them?"

"Oh, we have the top people in the consciousness movement — Dannion Brinkley, Lynn Andrews, Joan Halifax, Ram Dass, Chet Snow, Barbara Marciniak — pioneers in everything from medicine to Native American teachings to near death experiences. John Lear, for example is the son of the guy who invented the Lear Jet and he holds every pilot's license you can get in America. He speaks on UFOs too."

"Go on," I said.

"We have ex-military officers and physicists in the UFO field. People who were involved in the Philadelphia Experiment. People who are contactees and abductees like Travis Walton, famous hypnotherapists like Budd Hopkins, a whole range of experts."

How would I fit in? I was a commercial photographer in Atlanta. No one knew about me. And if I told them half of what I knew, would they even believe it? I had only just begun to explore my on-board UFO experiences through hypno-therapy, and I wasn't ready to reveal them to anyone. Besides, I hadn't been in the military and I didn't have a Ph.D.

Dee sensed my reservations. "You really have to do it, Tricia. Your information is too valuable. Your research on ancient civilizations, the origins of man, and how the ETs fit in with the larger puzzle is incredible. There's no one else like you out there. Besides, you're grounded, sensible and oriented toward helping people become self-empowered. People sense that when you talk. Time for you to come out of the closet."

I took a deep breath. What would happen if my family knew that I was speaking on UFOs? What would happen to my photography business if my clients realized I traveled around the country talking about multi-dimensional realities? Could I spare the time to be gone a dozen weekends a year? The constrictions in my chest told me I was very scared. What if I suddenly started talking about having Eagle-headed Angels show up in my bedroom? They really would think I was crazy!

"What's going on?" Dee asked softly.

I checked in with the panic. This was connected to a deeper issue. It had to do with those lifetimes of being killed for revealing my extra-sensory talents. And here I was once again, challenged to go public. I took a deep breath and said, "I'll think about it, Dee. Just send the papers in the mail." I could hear her smiling over the phone. Two weeks later she was promoted to Program Director of the Whole Life Expo, and I was officially invited to speak.

Breaking Free of the Fear

I returned to meditation the next morning, but my fear was so great that I could barely write. At last I scribbled. "Okay, I'm here. That's the best I can do."

Rigel cut immediately to the chase. "We know you are afraid of revealing who you really are."

The block that rose in my throat was immediate. For a moment I couldn't breathe.

"Do you not think that there are millions of you who are afraid to reveal who you really are?"

My mind was swimming. What did he mean?

"Do not think for an instant that you are alone, Beloved one. You are not. Every person on your planet is special and unique. Every person on your planet has a secret self they are afraid of showing. They fear that if that inner self should stand revealed, it would be ridiculed and doubted. They fear that if they opened their hearts and minds to their own great potential, they would be exposed to horrendous persecution. And why is that? Because it has happened before. It is etched into your historical past, etched into the memories of your causal bodies. The last 2,000 years were not called The Dark Ages without reason. Humans forgot. Humans descended into the lie of matter without honoring the power of their inner connection to Spirit.

"The entire system of consciousness on your planet has been based on conformity to the rules. You are not encouraged to step outside the lines and reveal who you are. That is how those who are in power stay in power. If you are kept powerless in your thinking - in the limitations you set upon yourself - then you are already a prisoner from within."

I shifted restlessly in my chair, thinking about all the people I knew who were pretending to be something they were not: corporate clients who put on their masks of respectability, art directors who were in constant fear of being fired from their jobs, musicians who forsook their own inner muses in order to play "what was expected of them." We all compromised our inner truth in so many ways.

"As long as people remain as sheep, or *pretend* to remain as sheep, nothing will change on your planet. It is only when they stand up for who they truly are that things will change. When one loves oneself enough to honor one's individuality, then consciousness will truly dawn."

I had never thought about it this way. All of us were afraid at some level that we didn't fit in. We had been brainwashed as kids to think there was something wrong with us if we weren't like everybody else. It meant we weren't "normal." We spent our lives trying to fit in. High School was a perfect breeding ground for this message. Special abilities were shuffled into the corner. Rewards were given for the status quo. The subtle messages we were given from the time we could walk and talk asked us to conform.

Messengers For the Light

A series of images swept by me. I saw the uniforms of our work places, the expectations of our families, those painful years of struggle with my house. I had been trying to fit into someone else's picture. Then the images changed like a movie. Mahatma Ghandi was standing before a crowd. Martin Luther King was speaking before the masses. John Lennon was singing "Give Peace A Chance". Bobby Kennedy was being shot for what he knew about the CIA. The women from the suffrage movement were being arrested. Chinese students in Tiananman Square were being murdered, and last, the crucifixion of Christ Himself.

These people had had vision. They had not had safe lives, but they had had lives that counted for something. They were not afraid to stand up for what they knew to be right, and they had changed the course of the world.

My reality was shifting. Suddenly it wasn't about me anymore. It was about us — all of us. If I had the courage to step forward, then others would too. If I had the courage to tell the truth about hearing and feeling and seeing Beings of great light, no matter how unusual it appeared to others, then the way would be opened for others to share their insights too. But as long as we all kept silent, I realized, we would remain the prisoners of our fears.

We would never know that the person beside us in the elevator had seen a UFO too. We would never know that the lady across the street had had an ethereal visitation from her dying son. We would never realize that our boss had a memory of being visited by an Angel when he was a child. Our real truths would remain untold because no one had the courage to speak up.

Tears sprang to my eyes, tears for all of us who hide who we are, all of us who are afraid to reveal our deepest selves. And it is because we are afraid to let others know our differences that we fail to realize that what unites us is far more profound than that which separates us.

"What do you want of me?" I asked in a whisper.

"We want you to step into remembering who you are. The centuries of torture have passed you now. The brutality of the Age of Pisces is fading. The Inquisition is gone. There will be no more burnings at the stake, no more guillotines, gallows or stonings. Many, many of the light beings on your planet suffered the blows of such ignorance, fear and superstition. It is over. And it is time to return your wisdom from the inner planes where it has been hidden and to speak it out upon the Earth.

"As a species, as a race, you are moving into another octave of evolution. That is why your brothers from the stars are here. Do you not realize this? The next millennium will bring your world into a circle of peace it has never known before, and we are here to usher it in."

"And how can I be of service in this work?" I asked humbly.

"Go into the world. As you speak of us, we will move through you. We will activate in all beings a remembrance of their own beauty. It matters not whether you speak of UFOs or Angels. Our presence is with you. As you stand in the center of our great Spiral, so will others know what it is to sit at the center of the Isness of Creation."

"But who are you *really*?" I asked them. "What is the Council of Nine, and how can you effect such changes with your presence?"

"We are the primordial wave forms which make up all of Creation."

It was Auriel. Her gentle presence descended like a mantle.

"We of the Council of Nine are part of the great circle which sits over the creation of this Universe. We create, maintain and sustain each part of it with the assistance of our Angelic brothers and sisters."

"And who are the others?"

"All in good time, my eager one. When you are ready, they will make themselves known."

"And Rigel? Where does he sit?" Auriel's smile was a benediction.
"Beyond the manifest realms. His is the deep primordial Intelligence that moves through my heart."

Auriel was Love itself, I had no doubt. She was the essence of the female aspect of God spoken of in the most ancient texts. Sophia. Mary. Quan Yin. The Heart of Hearts. And Rigel? Were there references to him as well? Or to the Council of Nine? Were there others who had seen or felt or heard of Rigel in any of the spiritual books we know on Earth?

I realized then that though I might know their essence, it was time for me to begin the next stage of my journey. I must begin the historical study of Angels.

Stories From the Center

Echoes of Forgotten Beings

Where did the concept of Angels first begin? Malcolm Godwin writes, "The evolution of the idea of a unique Angelic species can be viewed from countless angles. Historically speaking, they are clearly the hybrid result of an extraordinary Hebrew program of cross-breeding original Egyptian, Sumerian, Babylonian and Persian *supernatural beings*. This genetic interaction of ideas produced the outward appearance of the winged messengers of God which we know of today. By the first century after Christ, this essentially Jewish creation was adopted, almost wholesale, by the new religion and six centuries later by the Muslims. Since then, that fundamental angelic form has undergone no radical alterations."

"Supernatural beings ... " The phrase echoed in my mind. I opened a book of photographs on ancient Sumeria and caught my breath. There on the page before me was the image of a huge eagle-headed being like Rigel! Measuring some ten to twelve feet tall, this being was depicted in graphic detail alongside other humans — and all of them had four wings extending from their shoulders. I read the text below.

These were called Watchers, Nefilim or Annunaki — no one seemed to be sure. Long ago they came from the sky to help cultivate a large garden called E.DIN. Hmmm ... This was sounding extremely familiar. Could it be that this was our Biblical Garden of Eden? I read further.

Yes, the beginning of Genesis, I discovered, was pulled from a much longer telling of this tale in Babylonian and Akkadian texts called the Atra-hasis dated around 1635 BC[1]   And the Atra-hasis is taken from an even older Sumerian version of humanity's creation which was discovered in the early part of this century when Sumer was excavated in the 1930s.   It seemed that long ago, perhaps as long as 200,000 years ago or more, these large winged beings were involved in some sort of genetic intervention with mankind which resulted in our current species, homo sapien sapien being produced.[2] The Sumerian cuneiform tablets spell out these seemingly outrageous dates, yet modern archaeological digs are now establishing that current day humanity has been alive on Earth for at least that long.[3]

Evidence of Their Presence

I sat back in amazement. Here was *physical proof* that beings who looked remarkably like the form that Rigel had first taken when we met really existed. Was it possible that these beings were real? That they were not merely mythological creations? And if Rigel was part of a much bigger puzzle, why had he chosen that form to appear to me? Did it have some deeper significance?

I read on. These beings were referred to in the sixth chapter of Genesis as the Nefilim, which is literally translated in Hebrew as "those who had come down from Heaven to Earth." According to Sumerian cuneiforms, these beings had descended to Earth around 445,000 years ago. [4]

The Egyptians had another group of beings who looked remark-

---

[1] "Angels, An Endangered Species", *Malcolm Godwin, Simon and Schuster, (1990). 218.*
[2] "Genesis Revisited", *Zecharia Sitchin, Avon Books, (1990) 158-183.*
[3] "Forbidden Archaeology", *Cremo and Thompson, Bhaktivedanta Institute, (1993)*
[4] "Genesis Revisited", *19.*

ably similar. These were called Neteru's, meaning "guardians" or gods. According to most Egyptologists, the term Neterus or Neters refers specifically to the god beings like Horus, Annubis, Thoth, Sekmet, and Bast who visited our world long ago. All of these are depicted with animal heads, including Horus, who was considered to be an incarnation of God. To my surprise I discovered there were nine of them, a number that seemed to be reoccurring a lot recently. Hmmm... I wondered. Did that have some correspondence with the Council of Nine, or was it merely a coincidence?

In "Gods of the Egyptians", E.A. Budge writes:

One knows not exactly the meaning of the verb nuter, which forms the radical of the word neter, 'god'. It is an idea analogous 'to become' or 'to renew oneself' ... In other words, it has the meaning of god, but it teaches us nothing as to the primitive value of this word. We must be careful ... not to suggest the modern religious or philosophical definitions of God which are current today ...; neter appears to mean a being who has the power to generate life, and to maintain it when generated.[5]

Neterus, Anunnaki, Nefilim and Elohim are all beings who, according to history and legend, descended from the sky. Each of these groups is associated with the story of mankind's creation. Are they one and the same? We truly don't know. But if the Sumerian cuneiforms are to be believed, these beings were deeply involved with the evolution of the entire human race.

The Shining Ones

The word Elohim, like Nefilim translates literally to be "the shining ones who came from the sky." It is the plural form of a Hebrew word and originally appeared in the Bible in the first chapter of Gen-

---

[5] "Gods of the Egyptians", *Budge, New York, Dover Publications, 138-139.*

esis. "Then God said, "Let us make man in Our image, according to Our likeness".[6] What could the Bible have meant in using such a plural form of God? Examining the very word Elohim may give us clues as to who these beings were. Elohim has within it the key syllable EL, which means "bright or shinning ones." In other cultures this suffix, the singular EL "is an ancient word with a long and complex etymological history which has a common origin with many other ancient words in other languages." In Sumerian EL means "brightness or shining." In Akkadian ILU means "radiant one." The Old Welsh is ELLU or "shining being," and the English version is ELF.[7] It was then that I realized that both Rigel's name and Auriel's name had within them the suffix EL!!

I sat and stared at the pictures of these carvings for a long time. This being was clearly real. He had a feathered crest on top of his head. I didn't remember seeing Rigel with a crest, but still, it was an eagle-being, as Horus had been a hawk-headed being. Archaeologists, the book continued, called them genies, uncertain what else to think of them. This was obviously outside of their realm of experience, as it had once been outside of mine! What did it all mean?

As I studied their intricate stone forms, I noticed that great attention had been paid to every detail of the carvings. You could count the fibers of braiding on their robes. You could count the number of feathers in their wings, the tassels on their tunics and even the well-sculpted calf muscles of their legs. Someone had gone to a lot of trouble for just a genie!

Each Being, human and eagle alike, wore a bracelet that looked like a crystal watch with sections in it. Perhaps it was a communica-

---

[6] "The King James Version of the Bible", *Genesis, 1-26.*
[7] "Angels, An Endangered Species", *Malcolm Godwin, Simon and Schuster (1990) 36.*

tion device. Maybe it permitted them as light Beings to maintain a constant density at our frequency. I didn't know. Their muscled arms carried a basket, pulling fruit from the Tree of Life. Was this the mythical Tree of Life spoken of in the Bible? I was blown away.

Garuda and The Vedas

I was very excited by this extraordinary turn of events, yet I still knew very little. Perhaps there had been other beings of this nature who had visited Earth in other countries. And if they had left any records behind them... The mystery of Rigel deepened, as I asked the Universe to send me answers.

One Saturday morning I went to visit a friend. Bala was a devotee of the ancient Vedas, the oldest written literature on our planet. The Vedas originated in the East, and they describe everything from higher dimensional worlds to UFOs. My friend and I sat down to tea, and I began to relate my experiences with bated breath. After awhile he smiled. "Ah! Rigel sounds similar to Garuda. He is very famous in the Vedas."

"Gaurda? Who is Garuda?"

Bala stood, going over to a large picture book. He began to leaf through its exquisite pages. I went to stand beside him, amazed at the detailed paintings of these ancient epics. They were all Vedic stories. I was enchanted by the richness of color and detail. Finally he stopped at one of the paintings and pointed. There on the page was a being with the head of an Eagle and the body of a human. He had two wings, just like Rigel. I was flabbergasted.

"Who is this?" I stammered, sinking into a chair.

"Garuda. He was the companion and mount of Lord Krishna. Lord Krishna is believed to be an incarnation of God Himself." At my stunned expression, he added, "Garuda was quite a magnificent being."

No kidding! "What more do you know about him?" I said in a stunned voice. Bala smiled. "There are stories in the Vedas, if you want to read them. He was very wise and benevolent. If you want to know more you'll have to read the Vedas."

I went home that afternoon and asked Rigel. "Are you ... were you once Garuda?"

"Yes and no," he answered me. "Garuda is but one of many forms I take."

"But who *are* you?" I asked in exasperation.

"It will unfold as it was meant to. Continue your search, and you will find more than you ever imagined."

Thunderbirds and Kachinas

For days I wandered around shaking my head. What did all this mean? What was the synchronicity that would lead me to find two such beings in very widely scattered cultures? One night over dinner I was talking with a friend about my explorations and she said, "Haven't you ever heard of the Thunderbird among the Native Americans?"

Thunderbird? My fork stopped midway to my mouth. "Oh, you mean the Kachinas?" I *did* remember some of the beautifully crafted statues I had seen years earlier in the southwest. They had made no sense to me at the time, though I thought they were beautiful. I assumed that they were anthropological representations of a symbolic nature. Maybe I was wrong.

"You're right," my friend mused, "there is an Eagle Kachina, but the Thunderbird I refer to is beyond that."

My thoughts had not caught up with her. I was still lost in the Kachinas. Oh my God, there *was* an Eagle kachina! He had a human body, an eagle's head and wings! What could this mean? Was it meant to represent a *real being* that came to Earth? The similarity of this Eagle Being in Egyptian, Sumerian, Indian and now Native American cultures was astounding! Why hadn't anybody seen this before?

My friend was saying something about a Thunderbird. I must have looked at her stupidly as I tried to pull my mind back to her words.

"What about the Thunderbird?" I asked her.

"The Thunderbird is another name for the Great Spirit. He is the epitome of Divine Wisdom. He oversees the running of the Universe."

What??? I was speechless. What could she mean by that? Was there some real correlation with the being I called Rigel? What was I really dealing with here? Were there two things at work? First a race of beings — real physical beings like Garuda or Horus who had visited this planet in ancient times from some higher dimensional plane? Had they walked among us and taught us? Had they bio-engineered our race? Did they descend from some sort of cosmic bird tribe? And if this was so, were these only messengers of a more Divine Source? Were they agents of God? Did they belong to some higher dimensional planet of service and periodically go around and seed other worlds? And did they have anything to do with the being I knew as Rigel?

I finished my meal in stunned silence as my friend chatted on about Native American myths and legends. A New Guinea funeral ceremony, she added pointedly, also has a creature who resembles him standing at the front of their ship which travels to the other worlds. I shook my head in silence.

I hardly knew what would happen next.

The Council of Nine

The puzzle was becoming deep. A friend sent me a book by

someone in England who claimed to be channeling the Council of Nine. It was called "The Only Planet of Choice". I didn't read it. It was channeled material, and I was opposed to reading anybody's channeled stuff, especially in the middle of my own research. I didn't want it to affect the outcome.

Still, it was amazing that someone else was claiming to have contact with a group called the Council of Nine. If it was the same group, it might be a corroboration of the work I was doing. However, I wanted to get further in my direct understanding of these beings before I allowed myself to be influenced by anyone else. I would have to look into it someday, but not now.

Archaeological Digs and Bird Tribes

One afternoon I was opening mail. Someone had sent me a magazine from Australia. It was called NEXUS. I opened it. It seemed to be an exceptional publication, dedicated to the kind of in-depth articles on archaeology, science and forgotten historical finds that traditional magazines shove under the carpet.

"Thought you might like this," the note read. It was not signed.

Now who could have sent this? I opened the magazine to a startling article about the discovery of 60,000 year old petraglyphs discovered in an ancient canyon. The rock paintings showed hawk-headed beings with human bodies traveling in a canoe! Oh my God! I read on.

> Chambers Gorge, the site of creation myths in the book of legends ... is an ancient river valley ... deeply etched with ancient rock carvings, some of them strangely familiar and yet not an Aboriginal motif amongst them. Many of the highly stylized glyphs are remarkably similar to other ancient languages we have seen. There are figures with long pointed hats and falcon heads encircled by cartouches, along with a

remarkable carving of a helmeted figure with a bird's tale standing in a stylized boat similar to early Egyptian or Phoenician craft. Light box tracings from infrared photographs reveal the clarity and precision of the various 'written entries' on the cliff face. The archaeologist who gazetted this site for the National Parks and Wildlife says the carbon dating on the carving's interior indicated they are from a period 40,000 to 60,000 years ago ... and may represent the oldest rock art in the world.

I had to sit down. I started over at the beginning of the article and reread it slowly. The article spoke of the discovery of a stylized Eye of Horus, the legends of seven tribes "who came from the sky" to colonize Earth and additional carvings of stars and planetary motions which had been discovered nearby. It also said that the Eagle, the principal totem of the Aborigine tribe who lived in this canyon, no longer talked to the tribe because only one old man still retained the art of summoning the Bwanapul - those higher light beings who manifest through the vortexes to teach the people!

The Eagle! This branch of indigenous people was experiencing the Eagle as well. That was amazing! I decided to look it up in Barbara Walker's wonderful book, "The Encyclopedia of Myths and Women's Secrets". Under Eagle she had written:

Classic soul-bird, symbol of apotheosis associated with the sun god, fire and lightning. Greeks thought eagles so closely akin to the lightning spirit that they nailed them to the peaks of temples to serve as magic lightning rods.

Cults of fire and the sun made the eagle a bearer of kingly spirit; the god's soul returning to heaven after a period of earthy incarnation as the king. It was the Roman custom to release an eagle above the funeral pyre of each emperor, just as an Egyptian pharaoh rose to heaven on the wings of the solar hawk.

Horus! Whoa! This was astonishing!

I sat in silence with the book open. All of this was going some-where, but I wasn't sure where. I picked the book up again.

> The eagle was identified with the fire bird or phoe-nix, who underwent a baptism of the fire that "burns all sins" and was reborn from his own ashes. The eagle was the totemic form of Prometheus, who stole fire from heaven, like the eastern Garuda flew to the mountain of paradise to steal the gods' secret of immortality. Later, he assumed the golden body of the sun. American Indians had a similar hero, the lightning bird.

I shook my head in wonder. I thought about the Australian rock finds. They predated what had once been thought to be the oldest rock paintings in the world at the Cave of the Bulls in Altamira, Spain. Why hadn't we heard of this in archaeological magazines? I de-cided to go to the library. I checked out several books on ancient symbols. Most prominent among them was Egyptian. The glyph above almost every ancient temple or tomb in Egypt was a winged disk — the disk of Unity with wings.

Did these people know about Rigel? Did they know about Auriel? His movement was the spiral and the wings of an eagle was his symbol. Auriel's was the heart, the center, the shape of the circle. It was the vibration of unity. Did the ancient Egyptians know about these beings? And did they call him Horus? Why, I asked myself, would they use a winged disk as a symbol of God, unless it had something to do with birds or flying or freedom? I had a guess, but it was too incredible to imagine.

I went home and poured over the books. The symbols came alive to me, and for the first time I knew what many of the hieroglyphs meant. Suddenly a book fell out of my bookcase and onto the floor. I picked it up. It was a book I had had for many years and never bothered to read. "Return of the Bird Tribes" stared up at me.

I almost shouted. I looked around the room, but I could see nobody. Was someone trying to tell me something? I turned the book over cautiously. It had been written by Ken Carey. Had he been visited by bird-headed Beings too? I had heard that Uri Geller, the famous psychic, had been. Someone had told me that the first year I was with Rigel. They said that he had contact was with an eagle-headed being.

I turned to the Glossary at the back of the book.

"Bird Tribes," Ken had written, "the spiritual guardians of the Earth. Angelic entities. Human spirit or higher selves. Beings through whom the Great Spirit creates on the physical plane. Previous incarnates on this planet. Original creators of life."

I turned to another page.

"Thunderbird - a rarely used name for the Great Spirit, also thunder, lightning and rain personified as a huge bird."

Well, the plot had certainly thickened, so they say, and my guides had gotten my attention. I wondered what would happen next.

Human and Divine

 was entering my second year of speaking for the Whole Life Expo in cities around the country, and the pace was picking up. I traveled to New York, Los Angeles, San Francisco, Las Vegas, and a half dozen other cities to speak. And I had had a serious talk with my guides before I started, knowing that the practicality of being gone from my commercial photography business for so long would take its toll.

"If you want me to do this speaking thing, I will. But here's the deal. My business has to survive. You guys don't live down here on Earth where you have to pay rent and utility bills. These details are important, so if you want me to teach, I'll do it, but you have to send enough money to allow me to take the time off."

They laughed.

"Beloved, if you truly realize that God is everything, abundance in every form - the grass, the trees, the waters, the people, and the friendships that you form - why is it so hard to realize that God is also money? Money is man created, of course, but it is a symbol of the exchange of energy. We are that energy. What you are really asking for when you ask for money is that the energy of the Universe supports you, is it not? And if we can create entire worlds, dear one, money is not a problem."

Hmmm ... I'd never thought about it that way. "All right," I agreed with my best Capricornian practicality, "I'm willing to think about it in this way."

I heard the affirmation they wanted me to use clearly in my

head. "Abundance is in everything I do and see. God is in everything I want and everything I am."

I looked up to address them plainly. "And since you guys are working for God, this is going to be easy, right?" There was no answer. I guess they expected me to take their word for it.

Trusting the Flow

Surprisingly and effortlessly, this part of my life opened up. I found that as I traveled from city to city people would ask me to stay over for readings. I would go to the Expos, spend a week meeting incredible people, healing other's wounds, peering into the time track of galactic history, and making a little money at the same time. I loved it! And it felt completely right. Everyone around me was being accelerated in his or her spiritual growth, and I knew I was in line with my life's destiny.

I thought about those early childhood years when I had felt a clear sense of mission. I had known that I had incarnated for a purpose, known that I wanted to do something that mattered with my life, and for the first time I realized I was truly in the path of my life's work. Upon reflection, I realized that it had all happened when I was least expecting it.

Soon I was booked for weekend workshops speaking about Angels and Extra-terrestrials, two of the subjects that had most influenced my life. At these two and three-day intensives, I had so much material to cover that there was never enough time. I spoke on the "Lost Ages of the Planet Earth," "The Extraterrestrial Origins of Man," "UFOs and Ancient Civilizations" and the "Landscapes of the Inner Planes."[1] I created audio cassette tapes to spread the information for those who could not attend my classes. I realized, I

---

[1] *Available through Horizons Unlimited Productions, Atlanta, Georgia, 404-873-3070.*

just might have to write that book after all. In fact, I might have to write several. Many people, I realized, are tuned into either Angels or UFOs, but rarely both, because they didn't quite know how they fit together. I knew then that in future books I would have to write on both subjects.

After the second year of traveling it dawned on me that I could quit photography altogether, but I knew I wasn't ready. I was still attached to my identity in the commercial world, and I honored it because it grounded me. When people asked me whether I would give up one career for another, I couldn't answer. Both were part of me. The craft of "seeing" through a camera had its own rewards. It had been with me for years, and I was good at it. And it was but another aspect of my vision. When I shot pictures, I saw beauty everywhere I looked. When I did clairvoyant readings the core beauty of each soul I met was present for me in the room.

To Be Loved

Teaching about the Universe also forced me to integrate the lessons I was getting from Rigel and Auriel. That old saying about walking our talk is never so true as when we are standing in front of an audience, whether it be our own rebellious and adoring children or a group of skeptical strangers. We are all human and we are all Divine, and it became clear to me that the secret to self love was in accepting both of these parts of ourselves completely.

So often in our crazy mixed-up belief systems we are taught that we must be perfect to be loved. Nonsense! Each of us is eminently lovable even with all our human idiosyncrasies, and sometimes because of them. To be a teacher at any level is to accept the human part of ourselves, just as we must learn to accept it in others. This is the only way to love it into wholeness.

The time of the great hierarchies is passing. Classical religion and government has been adept at teaching us to put authority outside of ourselves, to place another on a pedestal. But to do so creates separation, and eventually those on the pedestal must fall, because they aren't being allowed to be human. And those on the ground will feel betrayed and embittered. I wasn't interested in supporting that system.

The Circle, I realized, is the form that is emerging and ironically, it is the oldest symbol of all. In Lemuria, the circle of leaders governed using that sacred form. In the Medicine wheels of the Native Americans, leaders met in a circle. That is how tribes were governed. And even our United States began with the idea of such a government with the Senate and the House of Representatives but got lost somewhere along the way of politics. In the balance of the Circle each voice is heard, and each person is honored. Each is allowed to be both human and divine. I was going to need to remember that.

Learning to love oneself in both these aspects, human and divine, is the most challenging task of all. We are our own worst enemies. The critical voice within us prevents so many from even imagining that they could be Divine. And all our conditioning has taught us that we are "unworthy" to even think of ourselves as eternal parts of God.

When I turned to my teachers it was Auriel that answered.

"Dearest daughter, w hat is it that you think separates you from the Angels? It is the knowledge that they have, and you have forgotten, that you are of Divine beingness. What do we mean by this? We mean that all things which are created have their life in the Eternal One. That One has placed the spark of fire, the spark of life, the spark of goodness within everything that lives - animal, vegetable, mineral, human — even those you would call extra-terrestrial. None are lost; they are merely learning different lessons.

Some do not see this Divinity within themselves, or even in others. Some will not claim it if they knew of it. Others dwell in the confusion of thinking that the light within will burn them to the core, that its all-revealing radiance is something to fear. We tell you this is rubbish. Each of you is Light. Each is lit from within by a perfect eternal flame, and within that tri-fold flame itself, you enter the home of my inner sanctum.

How can you find your spark? you ask yourselves. How can you love it? You can start by loving yourselves in whatever way you are - with all your sadness, all your heart ache, all your confusion. You can learn to honor the joyful differences that make you up instead of denigrating them by celebrating the shameful things you try to hide from others; by laughing in the face of that critical voice within; and by choosing to do each little act in God's name.

I consecrate my eating to God, even if I am over-eating in this moment. I consecrate my sexuality to God, even when my sexuality becomes an obsession. I conse-crate my bad habits to God, and I ask that whatever does not serve me be taken from me without pain. I consecrate my laziness to God, and I ask that my life will be given meaning.

When one consecrates one's life to God, one's life transforms. Start with consecrating the little acts. Do them in God's name. Then self-hate becomes God honoring. Self- criticism becomes self-accepting laughter. And self-blame becomes the detached spirit of patience.

You must begin to love yourself from whatever place you have started. And know that you are doing the best you can with where you are. Forgive and let go. Only then will love come forth to change your life."

Being In the Now

Each time I channeled for a group was an opportunity to

learn more about who these Divine beings were and what they had come to teach. Rigel and Auriel were never interested in facts. I was. I wanted to know about galactic history, cosmic science and a thousand details of creation. They were interested in the NOW. They are the most completely present beings I have ever met. At workshops they would only reference the past or future to illuminate the NOW. They were focused on creating change in the moment of celestial contact.

> "It is only by becoming completely present that you can hope to remember who you are. In doing so, you bring all of your multi-dimensional lifetimes together, your past, your present and your future. This moment is the perception of Eternity through the window of what you call time. For the purposes of change, there is no other moment than the NOW. It opens the path of the SELF to all possibilities. Be here with us now and we will lead you to the crossroads of your own self-transformation."

The Language of Light

Sometimes before an evening workshop, I would urge them to speak on a particular subject. I would hear them chuckling gently, as parents do with great affection as they cuff a beloved child.

> "Do you not think we know who is in the audience, Beloved, and what must be said to each of their hearts? We dwell in the province of that land, and the language that we speak truly has no words. It is part of the Language of Light from which all worlds were created."

The Language of Light? I had never heard of such a thing.

> "It is the primary language of God," they said, knowing my thoughts before I even had them. "The Language

of Light is the stuff of Creation. It is composed of light, sound and wave forms expressing God in manifold ways throughout every Universe. On each plane of manifestation the Language of Light may appear differently, as movement, sound or light. The music of the spheres which you have called the sound current is the underpinning template for existence as you have come to know it. There are remnants of ancient languages upon your planet, brought here by your galactic brothers and sisters, which still hold some of the integrity of the Language of Light. These are Hebrew, Sanskrit, Greek and Chinese.

Within the Universe, all form as you know it is created with sound. Sound allows light to manifest in what you believe to be frozen matter. But what is matter but the semblance of photons coming to rest within a given shape? To you they appear to have density, but in truth even they are vibrating with the language of celestial creation."

I thought about this for a moment. "Is that why you sometimes don't speak out loud when you come into my energy field?" I asked them. I was referring to a time when I had been asked to channel for a group who had heard me only two nights earlier, and Rigel came in to create a space for others to speak, yet only spoke a few words himself. At the time it had driven me crazy, because I felt the weight of expectation from those around me. He had laughed and said silently within me

"What makes you think that we must speak with words at all, when what we are is activation itself through wave form? Our role is not to be visible. We have no need of that. We have been invisible to all but the keenest of souls for eons of time. We have operated invisibly through every structure of your existence from the moment you were but a thought in the mind of God.

And yes, Beloved one, it is time for us to be known by the people of Earth again. That is why we are here with you now. Great change is coming to your world, and it is wise to be prepared. This change will sweep the Earth within your lifetime, affecting all forms of life upon it.

Humans have forgotten who they are, where they came from and where they are going. And it is time that they remembered. In knowing us, we hold up the mirror to themselves. When one beholds this mirror of the Self as God, then one begins the journey home."

"And what is the Whole?" I asked him simply. "Where are we going and who made us?"

"Bend forth your hearing, little one and I will tell you the story of Creation."

The Heart That Would Remember Its Name

Once upon a time, there was a Great Soul who looked into the mirror of Its deepest Self and let out a shout. It was a shout of wonder, a shout of excellence, a sound that seemed to have no beginning and no end. This shout shook down the corridors to make Time and Space appear. The mirror then burst into a hundred million tiny fragments, some larger, some smaller. But all gleamed with the same glorious reflection. And all held the image of the Great Soul emblazoned on the template of the mirror itself.

Thousands of years passed, then millions, even billions. The mirror itself had splintered again and again. Into the deepest, darkest crevices its slivers went, being buried in the playgrounds of Space, getting lost in the grid work of Time. Each of the slivers cried out, one to the other, yet each felt lost and alone, forsaken and abandoned. Some turned their faces to reflect light that shone from those orbs we call suns. Some found an answering glimmer inside themselves and polished their faces to look heavenward. Others forgot that they had the capacity to even bring light into the dark places at all.

The small golden sliver of the Great Soul's template grew dimmer and dimmer until it was almost forgotten, but not quite. For the template is the reflection of the Great Soul itself, and the call to return is the song of Love itself. This then is the Heart that would remember its name. When it does so, it will also remember its purpose. And to do either it must know that all splinters are part of the One mirror, and that all must return to the Source to be reunited.

This is the dilemma for two leggeds — to remember. They must overcome their belief in the illusion of separation from Source by remembering their Divine essence — Love. Separation from God or Source is probably the most insidious misconception operating on planet Earth today. This illusion is based on our forgetting the very place from which we started.

If God/Goddess/All that Is is the fabric of existence, it is impossible to be separated from It. And if Divine Love created the world, it is impossible to be separated from It. Do you not see? It permeates us. We breath it. Our entire world is made up of It as are all the stars in the sky. We ourselves swim in It.

"Ah!" you say. "There is no love in my life!" How can this be so?

Some may feel that they have experienced a lack of love in their personal lives, their work environments or even their romantic lives. Love has left them. Love has abandoned them. They are alone.

Stop. Look around you. It is not true. You are surrounded by beings like yourself who reflect light. You have only to realize it. Think for a minute how you have felt when you have been in love. Did you not experience the great expansive Oneness of happiness flowing through everything and everyone? Yes! And even though the world felt like it had changed, was it not you who had changed your perceptions, your aliveness?

There are two forces active in the world today. Love and the illusion that love is not, which causes fear. Of these two, Love is the only thing that is real even when we cannot see it or feel it. Just as the splinters do not remember that they are part of the One, still they hold light and reflect it back. That is their nature.

In the Lower Worlds of Creation, duality, time and space, male and female, perpetuate the illusion of separateness. Thus we see cycles of contraction and expansion in everything: the seasons, the tides, death and birth, fear and love. And all of them are only aspects of the Great Soul. And at the end of time only Love will remain.

The Language of Love and Light

Energetically Love flows out from the heart chakra in ever-expanding waves of ecstasy and pleasure, drawing one irresistibly into communion with all things in the Divine. And when one does not feel this Love in one's life what begins to happen? Perhaps one is angry, confused or hurt. These negative feelings form an energetic blockage in the heart itself. The flow of the Love current cannot get to you. These blocks can be thought of as tiny bits of debris stuck in the way of this free-flowing, infinite wave, blocking Love's passage both inward and outward, blocking, if you will, the very transmission signals from the Divine Source Itself.

The heart chakra then is the gateway to the higher worlds through the Language of Love, much as the brow chakra is the gateway through the Language of Light. The heart chakra is feminine and is linked with the Mother of Creation, She who first made the Worlds. From the center of the human body comes the key — Love. From the center of the human body comes that which leaps beyond knowledge into wisdom. The heart is the place of remembrance. The heart is the place of true knowing. In it, all tales become the One Tale, the story of the Heart that has remembered its name.

Yes, perhaps once long ago Infinity chose to have company. In this way, It could travel through Itself forever, unfolding in ever-widening circles, spirals and patterns of unspeakable majesty, expressing Itself endlessly through the unrepeatable unfolding of Its existence. Each of you is a sliver. Each of you has a heart that must remember its name if you are to be free. When one opens the door to Love, one begins to remember. One sends out a signal to all the other pieces of the mirror to unite, and only then can one begin to gaze into the Celestial Pond of one's own reflection.

Look! Only you may know its outline. No one may show it to you. Listen! Do you hear the WORD that cannot be spoken? Only your heart may tell it to you. Breathe deeply now and listen well. Do you hear the whispers of your name? It is calling for you to remember.

Castaneda's Eagle

 was in New York. One evening after a par-
ticularly energizing workshop, my friend Alan
Steinfield asked me to come by his apartment
for a few minutes. It was November and the
wind was brisk as we got into the yellow cab on 81st Street. Alan
and I had been friends since the first day we met in Manhattan two
years before. He is a terrific acupuncturist who had dragged me to
many a wonderful health food restaurant in Manhattan, trying to con-
vert me to vegetarianism. I adored him.

"I have something to show you," he said as we got into the
yellow cab. "But you have to come to my apartment to see it."

"Hmmm ... what is it?" I asked reluctantly, thinking of the long
ride down to the lower east side of the Village and back. "Can't you
just tell me?"

"It has to do with Rigel," he promised. "I have some clues about
his identity."

What? He'd said the magic words, and even though it was
late, how could I refuse? Besides, I was still exhilarated by the energy of the workshop, and even at 11:00 p.m. I wasn't ready to let
the evening end.

"Come on," Alan smiled mysteriously. "I promise you won't be
disappointed."

I knew Alan had been a long time student of many famous spiritual teachers in both the east and west. He had heard Rigel speak
only months before and recognized him as his teacher. In fact, Alan
had been trying to persuade me for more than a year to simply let

my guides do all the talking.

I had laughed self-consciously. "Oh thanks, Alan. That really makes me feel appreciated."

"Well, no offense," he said, "but they are heavy hitters. I want to see more of them!"

I shook my head. "Uh-huh. Sorry, you can't just leave me behind. Besides that's not the agreement I made with them. Speaking as a human being is every bit as important as speaking as a god. It takes both, remember?"

I recalled the decision I had made so many years earlier when I had channeled the Greek Oracle. Nope, the days of the unconscious channel were passing. We humans had to take responsibility for ourselves. We had to do the integration work as well. "They have to take us with them, Alan. Otherwise, what's the point? They've already arrived."

"But do you realize *who* you're dealing with here?" he insisted. "Do you have any idea of the *power* of these beings?" I didn't answer, and he squeezed my arm. "When Auriel brought the smell of roses into that room last night - - Wow! - were you at all conscious? Did you smell it? It was divine!"

Alan was talking about a small miracle that Auriel had performed the night before in the workshop. She had brought the smell of pink roses into the room during a meditation. She had explained that the rose was a flower that was based on the geometric principal of five, and like human beings and stars, who also have five points, they are a key to spiritual awareness.

"The rose," she had said, "is a higher dimensional flower which has chosen to remain on Earth. Its fragrance is intimately linked with the heart chakra. This pink rose that I show you is a reminder to love. It opens the heart. When you wish to heal your heart, or to touch another's heart, smell the roses. They will help you do it."

The cab screeched to a halt, and I was brought back to the present.

"I have some idea who I'm dealing with," I said quietly. "But they have to take it slowly with me, Alan. I'm the skeptical, stubborn kind, remember?"

We stepped out of the cab and he paid the driver. "Come on upstairs. I have something to show you that can't wait."

His apartment was at the top of a steep six story walk-up. He hadn't told me that. I was puffing as we reached the top of the landing and unlocked his door. It opened onto a little studio apartment. Moonlight streamed in through the top story windows and Alan turned on a reading lamp as we entered the room. I could see books scattered everywhere.

"I know it's not clean," he apologized, "but I love books and I've just run out of room." He picked one up off the floor. "Have you ever read any of Carlos Castaneda's books?"

"Yeah, a long time ago I read some in college. I like him a lot, but let's face it, Alan, he's obscure. It's hard to know what he's talking about because his language is so different from ours."

"Did you ever read "The Eagle's Gift"?

"I don't know," I shrugged, "maybe. Which one is it?"

He rummaged through his piles and lifted a book from the floor. "Look," he said, "sit down. This may be a little mind-blowing for you."

I put another pile of books on the floor and emptied a place on his couch. I took a seat. He opened the book and turned to a page near the end. "Do you remember when Castaneda's teacher, Don Juan, tells him what the true mission of a sorcerer is?"

All those books ran together. I couldn't remember one from the other, I thought. I shook my head no.

"Well, do you remember when Don Juan explains the Toltec

view of the Universe? What God is?"

Again, no. "What are you getting at? I'm not even sure I read that book," I said, looking at the cover. It had a huge eagle on the front cover of it. He opened it and began to read. "Castaneda is explaining what Don Juan, his teacher, has said about the explanation for the Universe. Just listen:

> The power that governs the destiny of all living beings is called the Eagle, not because it is an eagle or has anything to do with an eagle, but because it appears to the seer as an immeasurable jet-black Eagle, standing erect as an Eagle stands, its height reaching to infinity.

"What?" I said, grabbing the book, "let me see that." Alan turned the reading lamp so that I could read over his shoulder.

> As the seer gazes on the blackness that the Eagle is, four blazes of light reveal what the Eagle is like. The first blaze, which is like a bolt of lightning, helps the seer make out the contours of the Eagle's body. There are patches of whiteness that look like an eagle's feathers and talons. A second blaze of lightning reveals the flapping, wind-creating blackness that looks like an eagle's wings. With the third blaze of lightning the seer beholds a piercing, inhuman eye. And the fourth and last blaze discloses what the Eagle is doing.

A piercing inhuman eye! Could that have anything to do with the Eye of Horus?

> The Eagle is devouring the awareness of all the creatures that, alive on earth a moment before and now dead, have floated to the Eagle's beak, like a ceaseless swarm of fireflies, to meet their owner, their reason for having had life. The Eagle disentangles these tiny flames, lays

them flat, as a tanner stretches out a hide, and then consumes them; for awareness is the Eagle's food.

"Oh my God," I said snatching the book from his hands. This
was the same concept I had experienced that night when the light
particles ran through Rigel's body, only to be recycled by his immensity over and over again. Castaneda had explained it differently, but
then again, he was only repeating his master's tales. I had thought
of it as the Fountain of Life, because I saw that all things flowed into
it, and all things flowed out of it, as a constant recycling of life.
"This is incredible!" I said. "I know exactly what he's talking about in
this book! I've seen this, Alan, but it is much more beautiful than
what he describes here!" Alan continued.

> The Eagle, that power that governs the destinies of
> all living things, reflects equally and at once all those liv-
> ing things. There is no way therefore, for man to pray to
> the Eagle, to ask for favors, to hope for grace. The human
> part of the Eagle is too insignificant to move the whole.

That isn't true, I thought. It isn't true at all, but I could see how
someone else might think that about the Eagle. I had once wondered if God's love was impersonal, yet I had been experiencing the
most intimately personal love of my life since I had met these Beings.

> It is only from the Eagle's actions that a seer can tell
> what it wants. The Eagle, although it is not moved by the
> circumstances of any living things, has granted a gift to
> each of those beings. In its own way and right, any one of
> them, if it so desires, has the power to keep the flame of
> awareness, the power to disobey the summons to die and
> be consumed. Everything living has been granted this
> power, if it so desires, to seek an opening to freedom and
> to go through it. It is evident to the seer who sees the

opening, and to the creatures that go through it, that the Eagle has granted that gift in order to perpetuate awareness.

"He's talking about ascension," I said in a voice that didn't even sound like me. "Castaneda's saying that we don't always have to return again and again to the wheel of life, death and rebirth if we manage to realize our own Divinity."

"Yeah, but he believes that the height of any sorcerer's power is to sneak past the Eagle," Alan offered.

I laughed. "Sneak past the Eagle? You're kidding!" Why would one want to do that? It would be like sneaking past God. It would be like disregarding the very being which made life possible. It would be like avoiding the most incredible love in existence. It would, in fact be impossible!

"He obviously doesn't perceive the Eagle the same way you do," Alan offered. "But at least he knows that the Eagle exists, which is more than the rest of us seem to know. Do you think this is some kind of metaphor?"

I didn't know. I didn't know anything anymore. Everything that had happened was blowing my mind. "But look," he said, "there has to be something to this. It can't just be coincidence."

Alan was right, of course. Here, once again, was some sort of bizarre confirmation that I was dealing with extraordinary beings of great majesty and power, beings that others had perceived in the past. And like the Native American Thunderbird, this Toltec path of knowledge believed that God was an Eagle.

Well, maybe He was an Eagle ... or maybe he just appeared that way to those who could see Him. But why? I was a seer and I had seen him as an Eagle. Was there some reason that he took that form above all others? And if He, who was beyond the manifest realms, could take that form, then He could take any form. In fact,

He had. He had taken countless forms throughout countless ages. If everything came from God, then every form that existed, did so because of Him.

Why was this Eagle stuff so hard to accept? I didn't know.

Big Eagle Was Here

I remembered then something interesting that had happened a few months before. I had been doing a reading at my house for a pretty middle aged woman who had shown up with her adorable two year old daughter. I took them both upstairs to my meditation room, and in an effort to give the child something to play with while we talked, I had handed her two bags of brilliantly colored stones to play with. These were malachite and azurite stones that I used in my healing work. I set them in a bowl and put the bowl on the floor for the child.

The little girl, whose name was Carey, was delighted with the beautiful blue and green colored rocks, and she began to run her fingers through them with great excitement.

"Big Eagle," she said suddenly out loud. "Scary Eagle. These are big Eagle's stones."

I had stopped, transfixed. "What did she say?" I asked her mother.

"Big Eagle, scary eagle's stones," she repeated. Carey clapped her hands in delight and turned the bowl over on the carpet.

I could not believe it! No one knew that I had last used those stone in Los Angeles during a three day healing retreat I had held for thirty some odd people. During the final afternoon of the retreat I had done some intensive healing work with crystals. Rigel had come out and worked with these very stones for more than four hours!

The child's mother saw the stunned expression on my face and tried to explain. "Oh, she doesn't really mean scary, she means powerful," as if they explained everything. "She just doesn't know that other word yet."

"Is she saying Eagle?" I stammered out. How had this little two year old been able to pick up on Rigel's vibrations from merely touching my stones? And furthermore, why was she seeing him as an Eagle too?

"She's saying big eagle," her mother offered. "I don't know why. Does this mean something to you?"

Of course it did, but this woman knew nothing about my inner work. "Can you ask your daughter why she is saying that?" I asked her.

The mother shrugged. "Sure." She turned to her daughter. "Carey, honey, can you tell us why you're talking about an Eagle?"

"Cause these are scary Eagle's stones," she explained patiently.

Oh, I thought. I guess that was certainly straight forward enough. For some reason she had seen Rigel as I did, and known he had touched these crystals. From the mouths of babes, I thought incredulously. From the mouths of babes ....

Evidence of Things Unseen

*A*s our work grew, Rigel and Auriel began using my whole body during these sessions. They didn't merely sit in a chair and talk; they got up and moved around the room, stopping at this person and then that one. They would instruct or heal, encourage or transfer energy as it was needed. One evening after a particularly wonderful session, a Chi gong master came up to see me.

"Did you know that your guides are performing classical Chi gong movements when they speak through you?"

I shook my head. "What's chi gong?"

"It is one of the most ancient forms of energy balancing. I think your guides are trying to open your chakras more completely."

I laughed. "Well anything would help. I feel pretty small next to these guys. What does chi gong stand for anyway?"

"Chi is life - the eternal life energy, the breath, the prana. Gong means long work, so chi gong is the long work of eternal life energy."

"I should study this," I said realizing he was a messenger. I needed to pay attention.

"Why? The beings you work with already know it."

I smiled sheepishly. "Yeah, but I don't."

Radionics

I became increasingly aware of my own limitations in handling these energies, and I wanted to have some measuring stick to see how I was doing. The perfect opportunity arrived one Fall when I was attending a conference in Las Vegas, Nevada. I met a radionics operator named Don Ward.

Radionics is the science of measuring the calibrated energy of any living thing. Don did not know me or anything about my work. Thus, I reasoned, he was a perfect person to run the tests. Since I always like scientific experiments, I asked him if he would calibrate my energy output when I was in a normal state of daily consciousness, then again when I was doing readings, and last when I was channeling.

For those of you not familiar with radionics, it is a type of science that uses a machine which gives digital read-outs of one's energy fields in all seven major chakras, or energy points, within the body. A regular reading for any normal human being would be 75 percent to 100 percent activity in any given chakra. That would indicate that one is functioning well in that portion of one's body. These machines read directly from the auric fields captured on Polaroid photographs, since Polaroids carry both positive and negative film emulsions. The radionics machine gives digital read-outs in the five recognized human bodies: physical, astral, causal, mental and etheric, in each of the seven major centers.

Don knew nothing about me, and I wanted it that way. I intended for this test to be as objective as possible. He seemed to be a nice, rough-edged man in his late forties. He was interested in psychic phenomena and had been doing radionics for about a year. We agreed to take the Polaroids in his hotel room away from the distractions of the Conference where I could concentrate. He would then do the calibrations.

We shot the first photo of me in normal Beta Brain consciousness, and then one of my doing some clairvoyant work. Don sat down by the machine and inserted the first photo. The readings began. From time to time he would look over at me strangely and scratch his head. "Do we have the right photograph?" he asked after he had calibrated the second chakra.

"Yeah, I've got the other one right here."

"These readings don't make any sense. They aren't coming up the least bit normal."

I leaned forward. "What do you mean?"

He shook his head. "They're starting at 320 percent activity and going up. This can't be right. Here, let me try another chakra." He skipped down a couple of rows on the chart. "This is even weirder. Now the machine is saying 720 percent activity. Something has to be wrong. You just don't get readings like this from a normal person." He sat back. "Give me the other photograph." I handed it to him.

This time I watched as the digital calibrations began to rise again. 100 percent, 120 percent, 190 percent activity. It stopped. Why wasn't this one as high as the other photo? That didn't make sense. The first one had been the "normal" Polaroid. The one he had in his hand now, was of the clairvoyant work.

Don continued with the reading, watching the display climb to 316 percent activity. Both of us were confused. "This is too strange," he complained to me. "I've only had readings like this before when someone is channeling. And you aren't channeling. You're just doing a reading, right? And that first photograph should be lower than this one."

"I'm not channeling," I said, "but I am shifting from Beta into Theta and Delta brain waves. I've been tested before."

"But that doesn't explain the first photo. These readings aren't the least bit normal. I'm not even sure they're human." He looked at me as if he was joking, but I could see a glint of fear in his eyes. After all, we were at a UFO conference. Anything could happen. "You are human, aren't you?"

I laughed. "Oh, absolutely, Don, 100 percent, grade-A American. Of course, I'm human." After a minute I said, "I know what, why don't I ask Rigel to come in and you can take the third photograph of him. Maybe that will explain something."

Don stood up. "I wish somebody would. Okay, let's try it."

I asked Rigel to superimpose his field on mine, and Don took another Polaroid. It always takes a few minutes for me to come in or out of his field, so Don was well on his way to the read outs by the time I sat down beside him.

"This is blowing my mind," Don said, shaking his head.

I looked as the digital counter moved upward. 300, 500, 1000, 1500 percent activity. Without looking up he went to the next chakra. 1500, 1600, 1700, 1800, 2100 percent activity. "This can't be right," he said, standing up. "I hope my machine is not broken." He picked it up and looked under it. He pulled out the photograph of me and reinserted it. "Maybe its malfunctioning."

I was afraid to say anything, not wanting to scare him. "Wait a minute," he said pulling my photograph out. He flipped through his files and pulled out another Polaroid. "I know what this one reads. It's one of my baselines." He slipped it into the sensor array. "I've already measured it, so I'll know immediately if my machine is off." He pulled out an old graph and watched as the displays lit up. He began to scratch his head. "This doesn't make sense. This read-out is identical to what it should be. The machine doesn't seem to be malfunctioning at all." He looked at me. "I've never seen anything like this before."

"Well, Don, I think we're dealing with some pretty big guys," I said. "Would you mind if we tried the readings again?" Shaking his head in amazement, he slipped my last photograph back in. The readings began, chakra after chakra, finally stopping at 2900 percent activity.

He bit his lip in silence. Then he said, "Who are these guys you're working with?"

"I don't know," I said softly, "I'm trying to find out."

Who were they indeed? I realized then that Rigel had placed his own field over mine in that first photograph. The bottom two chakras had read .3 of one percent. If that had been my reading I would not be very functional in the physical world. In fact I might be dead. They had just been trying to get my attention, I guess. Maybe it was their idea of a practical joke. Well, it was pretty funny.

I said as much to Don. "The most amazing thing is that I'm not even channeling these guys to any kind of maximum capacity. I just wish I could get a real read-out on their energy."

"Well," he tapped his pencil on the desk deep in thought. "Listen, I've got an idea. We could try to find out what the read-outs would be if you *were* channeling them to maximum capacity. Are you game?"

My jaw fell open. Really? We could do that?

"Look, it's just an experiment, and it might not work; but I can ask the machine to give us a read out from the field of the Being that's already on the photograph. Wanna try?" We looked at each other like two kids in a candy store.

"Okay," I said, "do it. I want to know."

Together we watched as the display climbed into the thousands. At last it stopped at 39,000 percent. We both leaned over the machine and stared at it. "Holy shit!" I said, throwing my hand to my head. What was I dealing with here?

What was I dealing with indeed?

Behold the Face of the Divine

home in Atlanta I spent time alone with these thoughts. What was so outrageous, I asked myself, about the idea that God might want to take the form of an Eagle? Why had we so arrogantly assumed that God looked like us; like a bearded, white haired old man in Biblical robes? Why had we even assumed that God looked remotely human? Why did we think that higher dimensional life appeared like us? It could look like anything. I realized I was prejudiced because I *was* a human. I wanted it to look like us.

The Bible had told us that the Elohim, "those shining ones who came from the sky," had made man in their own image. Was the Bible speaking of the template of the soul itself? Or was it speaking of two-legged forms? Were the Elohim really Light Beings who could take any form they wanted? Did they look part human, part animal?

If God really is everything, then why couldn't God choose to appear to me as an Eagle? Perhaps the winged kingdom had attributes we knew nothing about. I remembered watching a golden eagle at a nature center one day and being awed at his majesty and intelligence. Maybe the hawks and eagles, owls and doves, expressed some master aspect of consciousness that we know nothing about. Perhaps they are more detached, more all-seeing than our emotional approach. Certainly the raptors, the hawks, falcons and eagles have the gift of sight. They can see minute detail from great distances, both close up and far away. That did sound an awful lot like the perspective of God.

The Dream

Then I remembered a dream that I had had many years before. This had been about the time that I returned from England. I dreamed that I was traveling across country from Los Angeles to Atlanta. I had managed to acquire an old beat-up paint box from an elderly woman who had died. The paint box was in the back of my car. All I knew about the woman was that she had been an Indian Shaman who had died and left this paint box behind. Somehow it had come into my possession.

Passing through Santa Fe, New Mexico, I stopped at a roadside rest area. I decided to pull the paint box out of the back seat and take a look at it. I sat down on the gray concrete bench, laying the box before me on the picnic table. I leaned with great curiosity over the box and lifted the lid. Suddenly a whoosh of wind came out of it, and two magnificent spirits emerged. I jumped back in amazement and was caught in the energy field of their power.

One of the spirits was a horse. The other was a golden eagle.

I was stunned. All I could do was gape in disbelief at the two of them. The horse stood beside me pawing and snorting. He was white and a dark dappling ran down his legs. His eyes were liquid brown and he seemed to be communicating, but I did not know what he was saying.

I realized then that the eagle had landed on my right arm. He was huge, somewhere between two and three feet high. His eyes gleamed with a brilliant intelligence, and the feathers of his body shone. I remember thinking that he was just too heavy for me to handle on my puny little arm, though I found him magnificent. After all, I reasoned, I had a photography business to run, and what would I do with such an animal?

"I can't keep this eagle," I said aloud to no one in particular. "What will I do with him?"

The spirit of the medicine woman spoke from inside the box. "These are your allies now. I bequeath them to you."

I protested. "Wait a minute! I can't do this! They're beautiful, but I'm busy. I'm a commercial advertising photographer in Atlanta. Where would I keep them?"

"They are yours," the voice said with finality. "They have chosen you."

I sat down in my living room, rubbing my hands on my forehead. I had forgotten this dream until now. How could I have forgotten it? It had been almost a decade ago, and the synchronicity of the whole thing struck me. It seemed incredible that a golden eagle would have been given to me in a dream years before I even met Rigel, but it had happened. Did this dream have some precognitive significance? It would seem so.

Indigenous people have long believed that the winged ones were emissaries of the Divine. Maybe they were right. Perhaps if God chose to manifest Itself in the highest form that we could perceive it, it would take the form of an Eagle. And who was I to judge, anyway?

Getting Down to Answers

I went upstairs to my meditation room and pulled out a pen. I lit a white candle and took the phone off the hook. I closed my eyes. I wanted some answers and I wanted them now.

"Rigel," I began, "I know you are the greatest Mystery in my life and my dearest friend, but I want to know who are you, really? "

I could feel his presence entering the room, and I knew this would be an important meeting.

"Are you a member of a higher dimensional group, some bird-tribe of ancient legend, or are you really something much, much greater? And what do you and the Council of Nine have to do with the Angels?"

His warmth flowed over me. I could feel the other members of the Council of Nine descending around me. They knew why I had come.

"We feel your impatience with this dilemma, Beloved, and we are not without empathy in this matter," Rigel began. "You are being asked to expand to an entirely new level of thinking, of holding reality, and this is most challenging for human beings. Is it not?"

I bowed my head in acknowledgment.

"You are a specific type of mammalian human, so naturally you want to perceive God as an extension of your human kingdom. Other beings in other galaxies have imagined God as well, and they too imagine the Universal Force of Creation in the form in which they were created. For them the Angels appear as reflections of themselves - luminous and self-reflective. This inclination among all forms of sentient life is but an echo of the inner knowing each of you has, that you are all a part of me."

"Ah!" I nodded. I had never thought of this. Perhaps for dolphins, the Angels appeared as winged sea creatures. What a concept!

"Let us suggest, Beloved, that it is the other way around. The human kingdom is but one extension of that which you term God. There are many others, all important and divine."

"Will you speak to me of life on other planets? I want to know about the   beings on other worlds."

His glow deepened. "Do you really ....? Then we shall tell you."

By the Vision Splendid

A shimmer began in the room and I felt a golden pyramid of light fall over me. Images began to appear.

"Within my body there are worlds within worlds: sub-atomic, macroscopic, microscopic universes that you cannot even begin to fathom. There are every sort of creature you can imagine: bird-headed people, cat-headed people, reptilian-headed people. There are small humans and large humans. Humans that are not even a foot in height and humans more than twenty of your feet tall. There are griffins and winged creatures of immense intelligence who use far more brain capacity than the people of earth have even begun to consider. There are masters of both light and of dark in the shapes of beings from your deepest mythologies."

"And what of the Angels?" I asked. "How do they appear?"

"There are Angels who look human, Angels who look geometric, Angels who are flaming bands of color. There are Angels of creativity, Angels of movement, dance and sound. There are Angels who bless a flower garden and those who hold the anchor points of time and space.

"There are mineral beings and plant beings and those who are the bridge between. There are plant beings who turn into birds and fly away and birds who become clouds and vanish in the atmosphere. There are aquatic beings who look human, who have visited your planet in the ancient past, and cetaceans who have chosen their forms so that they might dwell in your oceans today and balance your planet's harmonic field.

"In the worlds of my Creation, there are beings of such love and power that they inhabit the shapes of mountains and caverns, holding the vibrational matrix of your dear Earth in place with their inaudible sounds. There are those who inhabit crystals, rocks and streams, and if one learns to listen, one can hear their singing voices. Yeah, there are even beings who hold the fields of planets, suns and galaxies."

Is On His Way Attended

I was engulfed in the tapestry he was spinning for me. Within the pyramid they were a living hologram in my mind's eye.

His voice went on. "As one transforms the remembrance of who one is into total reclamation, one sheds the static nature of fixed form. What you have here in this dimension is the appearance of fixed form. But truly form is but vibrating molecules, and at more expanded levels of evolution, form and function become the same.

"What do you mean?" I asked him calmly.

"I mean that in all the Universe form is used to do a task, a thousand tasks, a million tasks. In the Angelic kingdom this is taken to the highest octave. Angelic forms are created to serve a function, to express the passion of the Divine. Some beings take form to seed a world, to light a fire, to move the wind currents, to hold a vortex. In this same way you humans came into being, choosing a form that serves the purpose of your dance.

"Behold the face of your sun, which is a circle. Is this not the shape of the very planet that you live upon? Both fire and earth take on the appearance of the circle, which is the matrix of unity completed. This simple form, this band of wholeness, is but a clue that they are in my service. Would you be surprised to know that they are Angelic beings in my service?

I shifted in my chair. Was he saying that planets are intelligent beings serving the life forms that lived upon them?

"Indeed. That is what I am saying."

It put a whole new twist on this idea of saving the Earth. In our world, most of us were just beginning to think of our planet as a living organism, something that was evolving in its own consciousness. Now I was being told that she was in fact an Angelic being in service to all of the people who incarnated upon her. *That* was self sacrifice!

"Have Angels come to Earth as human beings? Did they really take that shape?"

"The human form exists in almost every plane, in galaxies too numerous to name. It is what, upon your world, you would call "a popular model", but with much variation. Its finely crafted shape is used with much success, allowing flow of movement, agility and dexterity. It is easily renewable from the elements of creation, being made of carbon, which bonds easily with other substances. Yet in truth, it is only one expression that the soul may use. Do not imagine in your egocentricity that this model is the only one."

Images of two-fingered, three-fingered, four, five and six-fingered and toed beings appeared before by me — blue skin, green skin, yellow, white and gold skin beings; webbed feet, clawed feet, taloned paws, hoofed feet, feathered paws, furred paws, scaled hands, and human hands.

"Whatever you can conceive, I have created," and I knew it was true.

Such mind-blowing diversity in the Universe! No wonder they kept these visions to themselves. Would we even be prepared for it when human extra-terrestrials landed? I doubted it. The visions were mind boggling ... but oh so beautiful! I sat for awhile letting the stream of them pour over me, not wanting to interrupt the flow. At length, a beautiful rose-colored glow emerged from the center of the stream. It shifted into a hundred different shapes and patterns, at last taking the form of a human Angel. Auriel!!

Dialogues With the Angels

 pulled myself back to the matter of Angels and bowed to her. "And what of Angels? What form do they take? Do they always look human?"

"Let us see if we can show you," she sent through the radiance of her light. A blur of rotating dodecahedrons, tetrahedrons, spinning vortexes and pyramids flowed by me. "This is how light beings travel at the higher octaves of ourselves. We are light and sound and wave form, coalescing into shapes that you may recognize. We travel in spinning vortexes of our own light bodies. And in the essence of ourselves, form and function become the same."

Rigel's power spoke through the blur of shapes. "Form is peculiar to each Order of the Angelic kingdom. Each form is chosen for an Angel to serve the purpose of that Order. Some are human in their appearance; others are like nothing you would ever imagine. These forms may vary as the service of the Angel's work may vary. The language of the Angelic kingdom is truly the Language of Light, and thus their shapes may change as needed to give pleasure to your sight."

"You mean that we merely see them in human shapes?"

"Indeed," he nodded. "As you will."

"What is the Language of Light?" I asked them.

"On every plane, in every world there are remnants of it that remain. It is the wave form structure that descends from the first created Word. It is composed of three elements: movement, light and sound. The ancient tongues of Hebrew, Sanskrit and Chinese on your world are what remain from days when Angels walked your Earth. Certain extra-terrestrial races also know these codes, for are they not reflections of the great life pattern?"

The Music of the Spheres

The sound of music filled the space around us. I could not help but smile. Angels were suddenly everywhere in the room. I could hear them, see them, feel their energies.

Rigel spoke. "These are the song makers of my Heavens. They are the tones who sing the world into creation with their joy."

I laughed in delight. I knew the melody of these songs. These were the beings I had heard as a child by the spring. They were the same ones who had whispered to me by my altar, singing the eternal praises to the Creator.

"These are Seraphim," he said to my unspoken question. "They are the singers of the grid upon which all must breathe and live. They fill the worlds of our Creation, from the depths of many stations. Throughout my worlds their music lives, that they might love, that they might give."

"They're singing!" A great feeling of joy welled up inside of me.

"Indeed, they sing to all created forms throughout eternity. Throughout all worlds, my sweet seraphic beings sing, and they rejoice that they might bring the planes of manifestation into being."

The room had become happy and light. This was the first time Rigel had spoken in such rhyming cadence. I knew it was the Angels speaking through him, trying to convey something of their essence to my heart. "Rigel," I said, "I know I have asked before, and I will probably ask again, but who are you? Is it too much to ask that you tell me who you are?"

Truths That Wake To Perish Never

He smiled. "Ah!, what if I were to say that I am you in realized form, Beloved One? What if I said that I am what you will become when you have let your fears wash from you utterly? Would you believe me?"

My mind struggled with this. I always wanted explanations. That rational mind of mine could not let go. Suddenly, I made a leap in perception. Ah! Perhaps who and what he was was not as important as what I realized in his presence. Divinity. Love. Unconditional acceptance. Universal patience. Supreme wisdom. This was more important than figuring out the form he took.

Suddenly his wings were above me. They beat like the omnipresence of the wind, like the power of thunder, the caress of breezes. I felt myself enfolded and I surrendered to his power as it moved through me.

"Are we not all Divine Beings, oh my daughter, emanating from the heart stream of Creation. Yes, even humans unaware?"

The current caught me up. I was flying now. All that I could feel was the sweetness of his presence, like wings beneath my body. "It is the uncertainty that you fear. Let go and fear it not. Leave the mind behind. Leave it on one side of the chasm you must cross. It will always want a thousand more reasons to be persuaded to take that first step. And they will never be enough. The knowing is the experience, Beloved, and you do not need your mind or your ego to have a greater experience. Step out on the invisible bridge of inner knowing. You can always go back for your mind later on when experience has taught you what you really needed to know."

Suddenly I found myself in a place of utter darkness, like the utter comfort of a velvet night. It upheld me as I entered it, and instead of feeling like it was a vacuum, it felt infinitely full of possiblity. I was not scared. "You must go through the dark to find the light," I heard Auriel say.

In the distance I saw a spec of light, and at the speed of thought, it grew larger. I realized then that it was a great light, no, a thousand lights, a million — a million billion. More lights than I had every imagined in eternity. They were alive and glowing, tiny orbs and great large orbs, all sentient, all shining, spinning, bubbling in a whirl-pool of incandescent luminosity. The Cosmic Ocean filled my ears until it was deafening.

Rigel spoke. "These are my children, each and everyone, as you, yourselves are my children. Those whom you call Angels are the flowered blooms which sprang from my creation of the loom of time and space. The Nine were first, the primal race upon which all the rest is built. They are the template for creation, and in days to come you'll meet these first begotten of My will, and you'll love them as I do: Sabayoth, Metatron, Jockaman, Shekina, Levithan, Domalar. They each will come to you in time, as you are ready to receive them. And not a moment before."

Though Inland Far We Be

"Are we all Angels?" I thought out loud, the lights from the living river of souls reflecting off of me.

"Indeed you are, each one of you in a spiral of your own awak-ening. Angels are your elder brothers and sisters. They are above you in the spiral of eternal knowing - nothing more. They have em-braced more of the power and love within themselves and thus they are the messengers between myself and you — each one an agent of remembrance. They are the children of the currents — light and dark, servants to created whole. They light a star, they hold a world, they oversee each boy and girl. They weave the grids of time and space, and they protect each sacred place. The Angels are my dreams brought real, breathed into life upon the wheel.

"Each one of them is a co-creator in my service. Like your-selves the love and power is what sustains them in the end. They are made for it. They are made of it. Can you conceive of such a Universe, my love? That we so loved each one of you, that We cre-ated Universes for your pleasure?"

The thought was mind boggling. I had no words to say. I had never considered it this way. I had spent more than my fair share of time just trying to_get out of the physical world to a place where things were less stressful.

Rigel laughed. "Love all things in my playground, dear one. Bless each and every blade of grass. These things I give you: food to eat from, air to breathe from, water to bathe in, sunlight to dance in; each is sacred, every one."

I swallowed hard. I was humbled by the thought that it had all been placed here as a gift to each of us. I took so much of it for granted.

Our Souls Have Sight of That Immortal Sea

"Do Angels come to Earth as humans? Were we once Angels too?" This is what it came down to, I thought. We humans want to know where we fit in, where we're going. We want to know if we are really cut from the Divine cloth, or if we must earn it through the suffering of our journeys.

"Angels, like yourselves, are in a spiral of their own awakening, some more aware, some less. And like yourselves my dearest one, they serve my purpose by allowing life to be experienced. They set each galaxy and sun in place and are a mirror of my face. They breathe the breath of Heaven's gate into the worlds that I create. Their bodies are composed of Light, of midnight strands beyond your sight. Their music weaves the strands of time, beyond the knowing of your mind. They are my children who descend, to tie the knot to journey's end."

I closed my eyes and felt myself falling into the galaxy of liquid light. I saw myself as one of those countless orbs of luminescence and felt the tremors through my body as the reverberation of the Word went out into the furthermost reaches of time and space.

"Each of you is unique. Still each must make the voyage into the knowing of the heart. And for this trip, you have journeyed into countless forms on countless worlds. Right now you are a human being, giving birth to a new consciousness at the end of a long and painful era of darkness. Your world and all who live upon her, are about to move into an octave of light. And in that transformation, you will finally master those lessons for which you have come. These are lessons that cannot be fully experienced in the higher realms; the lessons of total balance between true power and true love. Both are part of me, as they are part of you.

"You too are Angels, unaware, do you not know this, dearest one? There lies the path to all of life. You wish to know who are the Angels? They are the heart dreams of Love made visible in my creation."

The Nine flowed around me in a helix-shaped circle. It was the infinity symbol! They interpenetrated everything. They were the molecules of everything I saw - invisible and visible. No form, no fire, no movement would exist without them. They were entwined to make up the matrix of everything we know as existence. I felt the power of fire, the strength of form, the wave of air, the nurturance of Earth and the pure power of beingness. I had a glimpse of what they were. To even descend into my presence was an act of the utmost benediction.

"I'm going to start studying the orders of Angels now," I told them with the greatest gravity, and they laughed as loving parents do with a favored child. It was Auriel who spoke.

"Go then and study what you will, but we tell you that you will never understand the true nature of the Angelic kingdom until you meet each Celestial Order, face to face, vibration to vibration, as you have met with us today. We raise our hands in salutation, and we bid you adieu in the name of the Council of Nine. You are always in our heart."

The Promise To Come

I placed my hands upon my chest and bowed my head. They had given me a great gift. I wanted more than anything to know them, to know them all. So in the years that followed, this is how my work unfolded - being of Light to being of Light as the members of the Angelic orders appeared one by one. And of course, this was but the beginning of the relationship between myself and each member of the Council of Nine. These stories, the miraculous tales of these incredible beings, I must save for another telling. And of the Angels — well that too, is another story, and perhaps it is best saved for "Beings of Light, Worlds in Transition."

But today my heart was full of all that they had shared, and I knew that change was coming to our Earth. Great change. Miraculous change. A glorious age of consciousness. And these great beings were preparing us for that next incredible step of realization.

Remember Your Essence

That night I dreamed of the Cavern Angel. And though it did not speak, it told me the future of mankind. The dream began in a kiva, a deep, sacred circle set into the Earth. It was an enclosed room with eight sides, one for each member of the Council of Nine, if you counted the center. Twelve other humans sat around me in the kiva, a blur of warmth and light facing toward the center. Through the yellow glow of candles pooling lambent shadows on their faces, I realized I knew these people, knew each one as if they were my own blood kin. Some part of me knew that though I had never seen their faces before on Earth, they were the brothers and sisters of my spirit, of the spirit which soared beyond this Earth.

I heard them singing, and I realized that their mouths were open in ecstatic song. Celestial voices filled the space around me, and I heard behind the human joy, the songs of Angels in the room. Their faces radiant, I felt the deep throb in my heart that answered theirs. It was as if our hearts would burst within us. I let my own heart's longing rise into my throat.

They have come from every star system: Sirius, Alpha Centauri, Andromeda, Arcturus, Cassiopeia, Ursa Minor, Ursa Major, the Pleiades, even Orion. From ancient times on planet Earth, from all the mystery schools of Gaia the members of the Brotherhood of Light came: Greece and Crete and Egypt, Africa, India and Persia. From Peru to Hawaii, from Europe to the promised land of America, these were my brothers and sisters from the stars come down to walk the

Earth path in their service to the Whole.

The Angel's songs grew louder. This is the future. This I saw. It was the answer to my question, "What will come of us? What will come of Earth in the years ahead?"

I looked around the kiva, trying to memorize every detail. The floors of wood were shaped into an octagon, candles dancing in the room. These people formed a family that I knew, time-out-of-mind, circle within the Circle. A place of deep beginnings, ancient endings; I knew them, each and every one. Across the galaxy, from cultures lost to human memory, they sat in council on our Earth. Deep in the bedrock of this density, they came for the love they had of our planet. These were the healers now awakened, returned to change the course of time.

They were all nationalities: Celtic, Indian, Jewish, European, African, Oriental, and Native American. They were the fulfillment of the rainbow prophecy — the Metis - the mixed breeds of the rainbow tribe. In every nation, on every continent, these souls were coming into form. Like me, they had been born in darkness, growing up hungry for a peace their souls knew existed long before they came to Earth. Like me they yearned. Like me, they sensed a purpose behind the madness of the world, and they had a feeling that something of importance was in motion. Perhaps like me they had been alone in a society that seemed oddly out of kilter, as if the customs of this world did not seem right or kind or just. And like me, perhaps they too asked to find a path of service to create a better world. If they were Metis, they would not, could not rest until they had found it.

Ah! They are returning, and in the years to come they will find each other on the Earth. Through hardship, joy and transformation there will come the uniting, and for this they came. For this they sing.

I looked around the room again. Six men, six women sat before me. I was the last, the thirteenth soul.

Ah! The number of transformation! Christ had chosen just that number with his twelve who had changed the world.

Within Our Midst

Our song spun out its joy and rapture and suddenly I saw before me a great and glorious figure. It was the Cavern Angel! She was majestic, tall and opalescent. Her gown shone white with luminescence. Before her face she stretched her hand, finger pointed up to heaven.

I gasped. This was the gesture I had seen so long ago in Stonehenge. With that one move the Cavern Angel had unloosed all the seals of the Akashic. My life had changed forever. Now, as I beheld this omen, I knew it was a prophecy.

What could it mean, that she was here, gathered in this sacred place? I felt a touch upon my hand. I turned. The joyful soul beside me smiled. He laced his fingers into mine. Without a word I understood. I slipped my other hand into the hand of the girl beside me, and she in turn reached out to take the hand of the brother beside her. Brother, sister, brother, sister, I loved them each and every one.

I closed my eyes and let the song sweep over me. Like Angels who have found their voices, our love poured out into the room. I felt the fountain of Light that moved within the center, flowing out from the core like a spray of moving fireworks. I opened my mouth and sang the words.

The vision of the Cavern Angel turned in slow motion before me.

In this holy place and time
We meet again on holy ground.
From all the corners of the Earth
We have been lost,
and now are found.
In this circle of salvation,
In this crevice of rebirth,
We come united to the promise
That Love is coming to the Earth.
Sing sweet you children of tomorrow
Sing out your joy in every part
Lift high your love with all the angels
Who bless you in their heart of hearts.
Will the circle go unbroken?
Will the children now be free?
At last the words have now been spoken.
Great peace and love abide with thee.

The Cavern Angel held me spellbound. And suddenly I heard her.

"When you of Earth are gathered in this circle, in the circle of Truth, and peace and purpose, when as a world and as a people, you behold each other's faces with the knowing of the heart, then all the veils between you and heaven will be lifted, and you will remember who you are. The global family is awakening. The galactic family has arrived. Angels above you. Angels below you. Heal the Earth, and heal yourselves."

It was a prophecy, this I knew. And in my lifetime I would live to see it come to fruition. The Dove alighting, the Earth uniting.

The words of my guides came back to me. "When you are ready, truly ready, to come into Remembrance of the Heart, then you may start your journey home again." Ah sweet Rigel, Auriel ... beloved counsel to my spirit.

I closed my eyes and took a breath. If I was still, so very still, I could hear the Universe singing.

Acknowledgements

There are many human beings that have graciously helped with the birthing of this book. I wish to thank all of them. My dear friends Lisa Rubarth, Lorie Marcus, Brit Nelson, Josie Bitner, Cathy Brilliant, David Richards, Marc Shroetter, Leslie Sherman, Dan Liss and Mark Woodhouse for listening and encouraging this work with love. Karen Willis for editing, Greg Waters for design and Gary Bonnell for magically appearing at the right moment for production and advice . Last, but certainly not least, the kind hearted Eric Bergerson for all his legal miracles. Thank you, thank you all from the bottom of my heart.

About the Author

Tricia McCannon is an American mystic, historian, and clairvoyant. She travels and speaks internationally on UFOs, multi-dimensional realities, shamanism, healing the Earth, and the nature of the Angelic worlds. She is initiated as a Priestess of Isis, trained in the science of soul travel, and is a Christian (albeit the expanded version). She lives in Atlanta, Georgia and can be reached through

Horizons Unlimited Productions, Inc.
931 Monroe Drive
Suite 102 - #329
Atlanta, GA 30308

Order Form

Fax Orders: 404 873-3128   **Telephone Orders:** 888 873-6682
          404 876-4442   404 873-3070
          Http://www.planetlink.com/intergalactic

Postal Orders: Horizons Unlimited Productions
          931 Monroe Drive, Suite 102 - #329
          Atlanta, Georgia 30308

"Dialogues With the Angels" $13.95 + $3.50 ea.
230 pages paperback

"UFOs in America in the Coming Millennium" $20 + $3.50 ea.
Modern day history of Amercia's involvement
and a worldwide overview of UFOs
and their impact now
(3 hour audio tape) original music
(1 1/2 hour video with slides) $25 + $3.50 ea.

"UFOs and Ancient Civilizations" $20 + $3.50 ea.
Greek, Roman, Mayan, Egyptian involvement
with UFOs and an understanding of time through
the Procession of the Equinoxes
(3 hour audio tape) original music

"Landscape of the Inner Planes" $20 + $3.50 ea.
Near death, out of body experiences,
the Tibetan and Egyptian Books of the Dead,
the holographic universe and a meditation
(3 hour audio tape) original music

Payment: Credit Card: ☐ Check payable to Horizons Unlimited Prods.
             Name on card: _____
             Card number: _____ Exp. Date:_____

Signature: _____

Send to: Name_____
           Address _____
           City/State _____ Zip _____